Published by
FORMING LIVES INC

Copyright © 2020 by
GOOD WORD TRUST

Title
MY BEST ME - Teacher Guide 3

Editor-In-Chief
Josien Knigge

Authors
Amy Nevares
Elizabeth Palmer Solon
Anne Marie Wahls
Josien Knigge

Editor
Virdeen J. Muñoz

Revision and Correction
Josien Knigge

Technical Editor
Carlos A. Ferrufino

Cover Design
Ziza Zoe Malloy

Special thanks to Dr. Chan Hellman and
the OU-Tulsa Hope Research Center
for their curriculum content review.

HOPE RESEARCH CENTER
The UNIVERSITY of OKLAHOMA - TULSA

ISBN-13: 978-1-951061-18-0

Hope Rising SEL
PO Box 722255
Norman, OK 73070
United States
Tel: (405) 676-4140
Mail: info@hoperisingsel.com
www.hoperisingsel.com

MW01241834

My Best Me is a series of lessons designed to help young people discover their true identity and purpose. Hope delivered through social emotional learning (SEL) enhances students' cognitive competence giving them the integrated skills needed to deal effectively and ethically with daily tasks and challenges. My Best Me integrates intra-personal and interpersonal conversations around five core competencies and seven principles. Student participation, uninterrupted classroom instruction and a superior learning environment are the returns on time invested in hope.

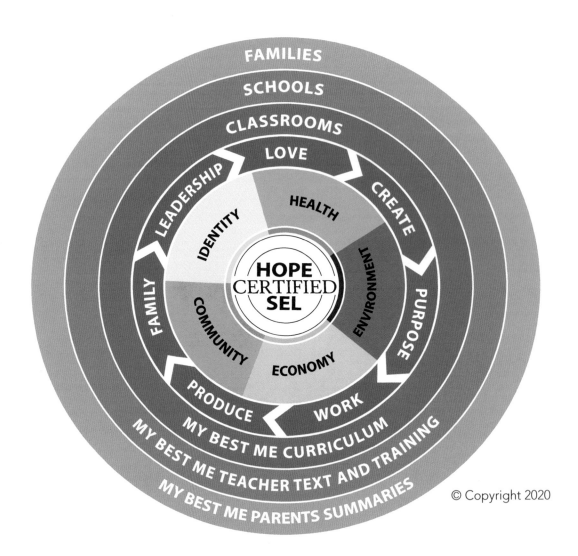

© Copyright 2020

teamwork • willpower • leadership • goal setting • growth mindset • problem solving
time management • reasoning skills • organizing skills • strategic thinking • conflict resolution
willingness to learn • creative thinking • stress management • finance management
communication skills • emotional intelligence • nonverbal communication

The Science and Power of Hope
What Our Research Shows

What is Hope?
Hope is the belief the future will be better than today, and you play a role in making that future possible. Hope is not a wish. Hope allows us to identify valued goals, set the pathways to achieve these goals, and exert the willpower to make these goals possible.

Can Hope Be Measured?
We published two meta-analytic studies on the Children's Hope Scale and the Adult Hope Scale. These publications provide strong evidence in the validity and reliability of the scales used to measure hope. This research is informing the field that hope scores can be used with confidence for both researchers and practitioners.

Can Hope Be Learned?
This line of research identifies strategies to nurture hope among those experiencing trauma and adversity. Hope is malleable across the life span showing that targeted program services can help move from despair to hope for both children and adults. This research is guiding our work to identify effective practices and develop training programs for service providers.

Impact of Hope on Trauma Survivors:
These publications provide a framework for organizations to become trauma informed and hope centered when working with survivors. Incorporating strategies to nurture hope leads to positive outcomes. This research provides a unifying framework that can shape advocacy and social policy around hope's evidence-based practice.

Impact of Hope on Education Outcomes:
Hope is linked to positive outcomes and important assets:
  - ➤ Well-Being
  - ➤ Education: Comparing Lower Hope to Higher Hope Students:
    - ➤ Lower Suspension/Expulsion (68% to 91%).
    - ➤ Lower Dropout (81%).
    - ➤ Lower Chronic Absenteeism (44%).
    - ➤ Higher Grades.
    - ➤ Higher Graduation Rates.

Chan Hellman PhD

Chan joined the University of Oklahoma in 2002. Chan is a professor in the Anne & Henry Zarrow School of Social Work and Founding Director of the Hope Research Center. He also holds Adjunct Professor appointments in the OU College of Public Health and School of Community Medicine.

Chan has numerous scholarly publications and books and has presented his research at both national and international conferences. Chan teaches both the master's and doctoral level primarily in the areas of positive psychology, research methods, and statistics.

Chan's current research is focused on the application of hope theory to predict adaptive behaviors and hope as a psychological strength that buffer stress and adversity among those impacted by family violence. In this context, he is also interested in the impact of prevention and intervention services on improving hope and well-being. Chan has also begun to examine the effects of collective hope on a community's capacity to thrive.

Schools and classrooms are increasingly filled with children exposed to trauma. Awareness of the impact on the learning environment is increasing and teachers, counselors, and administrators are asking for strategies to work with trauma exposed children. I consistently hear from teachers, that what they need are the tools to mitigate this trauma so that all children in their classroom have the opportunity to thrive. After more than a decade of scientific research, I am convinced that hope is the answer. Children need hope perhaps now more than ever before.

I have been publishing peer-reviewed scientific research studies that demonstrate the simple process to nurture hope in children, youth, and adults. Our research studies have even focused on the impact of hope on children with high trauma experiences such as those described in the Adverse Childhood Experiences (ACE) literature. We have consistently found that nurturing hope in children not only improves their academic performance, but that hope is an important coping resource protecting children from adversity and stress. The science of hope is well-established, demonstrating that hopeful children do better.

Hope is the belief that the future is going to be better than today and that I have the power to make it happen. Hope is not a feeling, but a way of thinking about the future and how you can begin achieving your goals. Hope is the ability to set goals, identify the pathways to achieve those goals, and the capability to focus mental energy (agency) to those pathways. Hope is not wishful thinking, rather, hope is about taking action to pursue your goals. The simplicity of hope is that it is about helping children set goals and finding the pathways and motivation to pursue those goals. The science of hope shows that a child's hope score predicts better grades, attendance, and graduation rates. Classrooms with higher hope children perform better in terms of chronic absenteeism, truancy, drop-out rates, academic achievement, and graduation rates, even when controlling for socioeconomic status. Children with higher hope are better at self-regulating their thoughts, emotions, and behaviors. They are better at setting goals, finding pathways, problem solving, and sustaining the willpower to pursue their goals even when faced with barriers and adversity. Hopeful children have better academic engagement as well as overall well-being. As an added bonus, the science of hope shows that teachers with higher hope are better at finding strategies to reduce burnout and stress so that they may thrive as well.

Hope is good for everyone and is grounded in science. Here is the good news!

1. Hope is a protective factor against anxiety and stress.
2. Hope leads to good outcomes.
3. Hope can be taught and learned.

Improving Hope
Through My Best Me

The really exciting news is that hope can be improved through simple learning strategies like those developed in the "My Best Me" curriculum. This research-based curriculum can increase the social and emotional skills that will help nurture and support hope in your classroom. As you go through the curriculum with your students, you will see a greater level of goal setting, pathways development, and sense of agency that is necessary for children to thrive both in and out of the classroom.

As you start to use *My Best Me* to empower students to build their HOPE, here are suggestions for you to begin to build HOPE.

1. To begin this process, start by highlighting core values.
   - Shift the message from avoiding negative behaviors, to achieving what is valued.
   - Discuss the definition of hope and how it differs from wishful thinking.
   - Connect each individual to a greater sense of belonging and achievement.

2. Practice short-term goal setting.
   - Trauma exposed children are much better at short-term thinking.
   - List the short-term benchmarks as steps toward your goal.
     1. What can you do this week, today, this hour, this moment?

3. Actions should be inspirational. Pathways that clearly connect to the goal are motivating and show children that their future is possible.

4. Set up processes to capture and share stories about **hope heroes**, people who find creative solutions to barriers to achieving their dream. (Hope Modeling).

5. Stay connected: Hope is a social gift that is nurtured through relationships.

6. When we experience adversity, trauma leads us to worry about the future or ruminate on the past. When our attention is focused on worry or rumination, we cannot be enthusiastic about the future.

7. Hope is a candle in the darkness. Create a Hope Map or simple visual to communicate hope to others.
   - Use pictures or symbols that provide a visual for goals, pathways, agency that can be displayed in the classroom.
   - Visual maps are a daily reminder that our future is possible

To learn more about HOPE, how it is measured, and strategies to nurture in children and adults, read *HOPE Rising, How the Science of HOPE Can Change Your Life* by Casey Gwinn, J.D. and Chan Hellman, Ph.D.

Contents

 Identity

Health

Community

Environment

Economics

Understanding the Icons

 READn

A story, a poem, a saying or a script that adds to the subject

 UNDERSTAND

To obtain knowledge, insight, and understanding through information

 OBSERVE

To look, see, find, watch, and discover more

 CREATE

To paint, color or make in a personal manner

 GAME

Engage in an experience and discovery together

 WRITE

To write, mark, or sketch personal ideas or discoveries

 CONCLUSION

A closing statement on the lesson subject with a final thought

 APPLY

To bring into action, put to use, and demonstrate understanding

 GIFT

A contribution, present or surprise to share with others

 ACTIVITY

A task that involves direct experience and action

 COMMENT

Discuss, consider, or examine certain subjects

 REFLECT

Think, ponder, meditate or wonder about important issues

 MUSIC

To learn, write, sing or listen to a song; enjoy a harmony of sounds

 VIDEO

Watch a clip or film section and analyze the information

Lesson 1

Materials
My Best Me textbook, writing utensils, journal, audiovisual equipment, rocks for decorating, art supplies for painting and decorating the rocks

Resources
<u>Introduction Parent:</u> 4yu.info/?i=98540
<u>Student Worksheet:</u> 4yu.info/?i=983010
<u>Parent Summary:</u> 4yu.info/?i=98351
<u>Student Pledge:</u> 4yu.info/?i=98541
<u>Video:</u> Hope Works - 4yu.info/?i=93011

Glossary
social emotional learning, adversity, measurable, predicts, sensations, resentment, apathy, remorse, confidentiality

Motivation
Hope is the belief that the future is going to be better than today and that each of us, personally, have the power within us to make it happen. Hope is not a feeling, but a way of thinking about the future and your role in achieving your goals. Hope is the ability to set goals, identify the pathways to achieve those goals, and the capability to dedicate the mental energy (agency) to acting on those pathways and reaching your set goals. Hope is not wishful thinking; rather, hope is about taking action to pursue your goals.

The simplicity of hope is that it is teachable and, therefore, measurable. It is about setting goals and finding the pathways and motivation to pursue those goals. (Goals, Pathways, and Agency).

When we understand that increased hope levels predict greater and better outcomes of success and that the steps to increasing our hope are so simple, hope should arise. *My Best Me* is a tool in your hand to support your students in building their hope through a social emotional learning process.

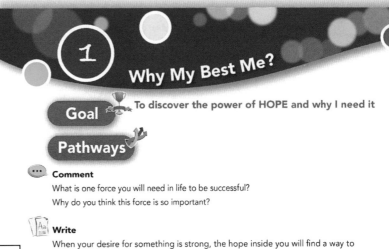

1
Why My Best Me?

Goal To discover the power of HOPE and why I need it

Pathways

Comment
What is one force you will need in life to be successful?
Why do you think this force is so important?

Write
When your desire for something is strong, the hope inside you will find a way to realize that desire. Want + Way + Will = Wellbeing.
Look at page 3 and fill in the words that are used for

Want: __ __ __ __ __
Way: __ __ __ __ __ __ __ __
Will: __ __ __ __ __ __ __ __ __ __
Wellbeing: __ __ __ __

Understand
Hope is a very important power within you, because it helps you believe in a better tomorrow, no matter what. It also helps you speak about a better tomorrow, plan for a better tomorrow and then, take actions toward that better tomorrow.

Activity - Let's Rock the World
Select a rock; one that you found or a rock your teacher offers you. Decorate your rock into a beautiful reminder of inspiration for when times are hard and difficult. Your rock will be part of

10

Goal

This is an introduction to the *My Best Me* textbook. The focus is to build hope through a social emotional learning process

Pathways

Comment: Students need the force called hope to advance and be successful in life. Hope is an inner drive that makes individuals press in to changing the circumstances of their life. Students can learn to adjust their mindset using hope and realize that hope is the single most important element for change to happen in their life on a short term basis as well as a long term basis. Hope is something that is within their control. They will need to learn to take the simple steps addressed in the lesson.

the classroom "rock garden" with the purpose of encouraging you and your classmates to believe that anything is possible.

Apply

These lessons talk about very personal things or what we would call private information, like dreams, beliefs, fears, pains, struggles, and much more. It is important that each student avoids talking about what other classmates share. Your teacher will ask everyone in your class to sign a Confidentiality Agreement. That means that everyone promises to actively participate in class, be kind, thoughtful, trustworthy and wise. You are encouraged to sign this Confidentiality Agreement as a pledge to your peers and teacher that you are will always help build hope.

Video: 4yu.info/?i=93011

Watch this video to understand how small things can have a king-size impact. It will give you hope as you discover how important you are and how the world is waiting for your ideas.

4yu.info/?i=93011

Reflect

Here are some very important pieces to the HOPE puzzle:

1. You need to feel loved and valued. Who really loves you?
2. You need to know who you are. What makes you so special?
3. You need to know why you are alive. What can you give to help someone else?
4. You need to feel you belong somewhere. Where do you fit in?
5. You need to know you can become anything you want. What is something you dream of being or doing?

Willpower

Hope is my anchor. It helps me set goals, find pathways, grow my willpower and succeed.

11

Write: Students will be encouraged to go to pages 2 and 3 in their *My Best Me* textbook and discover what the 4 words in this lesson stand for: The WANT is to set a goal, the WAY is to find pathways, the WILL is to build willpower and the WELLBEING is hope or the confidence in a better tomorrow.

Understand: Because we are addressing social emotional learning, do not be taken by surprise that a variety of emotions will surface in some or maybe all or your students and that social frictions might occur during some of these lessons. You might want to "measure the mood" before you start these lessons with a simple activity, where students let you and the class know where they are emotionally in their life. You can do this with emojis, words, color or even actions. Choose 5 faces, words, colors or actions that are standard in your classroom which students can use to indicate their mood. (The classroom can help you decide and create the 5 mood signals to use during

the day.) Have students lay the face, word, or color on their desk and take a moment to walk by each desk, look your student in the eyes and recognize their signal for the mood they are in. If they indicate their mood with an action, let them greet you a certain way (previously established) as you walk by their desks. If you sense possible frictions, take actions to set up your class in such a manner that you will be able to manage your students and their reactions.

Activity: Have your students create a rock garden or basket for the classroom with the encouraging, inspirational and motivating rocks your students made. These rocks can be used when one of your students needs a lift-me-up moment.

Apply: Because of the sensitive issues that will be addressed and the information shared, a Confidentiality Agreement (or student pledge) has been attached (see link: 4yu.info/?i=98541). The document can be printed and students can be invited to sign and commit to being a trustworthy classmate.

Video: Have your students watch this beautiful video showing that hope works. It is inspirational and shows that we can reach each other, encourage each other and help each other build a better tomorrow. Review the video with your class by asking them for their thoughts on the video.

Reflect: This is an opportunity for students to contemplate and answer these questions, building their willpower to find the pathways in pursuit of their goals. These questions should cause them to realize their life is valuable and precious.

Willpower

Students should have already increased their hope by going through this lesson. It is a simple three step process with huge positive impact and change: set goals, identify pathways and develop willpower.

Lesson 2

Materials
My Best Me textbook, writing utensils, journal, paper, encourage students to bring in family photos, or have parents email pictures to you, access to Internet and printer to print images

Resources
Student Worksheet: 4yu.info/?i=98302
Parent Summary: 4yu.info/?i=98352
Article: Building Successful and Strong Family Bonds - 4yu.info/?i=93022

Glossary
common, role, instructions, bond, compare

Motivation
Students will discover that the world is a melting pot of various family structures. The uniqueness of a family varies by its values, cultural norms, personal beliefs and/or life experiences. Discussing family structures with students can be a sensitive issue. Nevertheless, it will encourage them to identify the special characteristics of their own family and help them understand that no two families are exactly alike. Learning about families will enable students to accept families that appear to be different than their own.

Students can also dream and describe their own future family, defining features they believe to be important. Attached is an article on the 5L's of building successful and strong family bonds 4yu.info/?i=93022
1. **Learn values**, what significant, meaningful beliefs does the family unit stand for
2. **Loyalty** unites the family as they serve each other in all of life's situations
3. **Love** bonds the family together and stimulates the development of its member's
4. **Laughter** brings relief and balance into relationships, helping each member look at life from a more positive point of view.
5. **Leadership** motivates members to work together as a team, using their strengths for the betterment of each individual.

These 5L's can guide the students to evaluate their family relationships. They can share how these operate in their family and hear about other families.

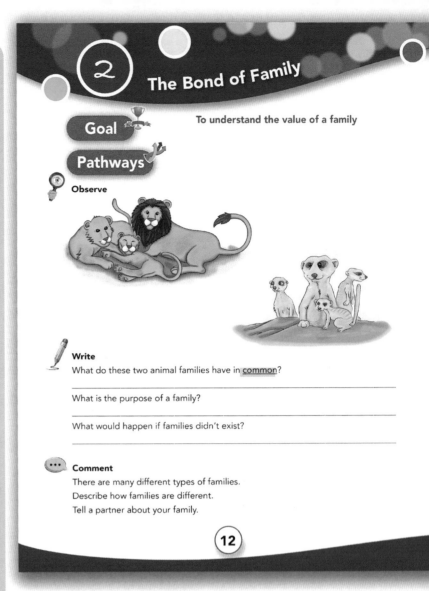

Goal
To understand the value of a family

Pathways

Observe

✏️ **Write**
What do these two animal families have in <u>common</u>?
_____
What is the purpose of a family?
_____
What would happen if families didn't exist?
_____

💬 **Comment**
There are many different types of families.
Describe how families are different.
Tell a partner about your family.

12

Goal
To recognize and appreciate their family and understand different family units and how they function and operate

Pathways

🔍 **Observe:** The images show animal families. Have students express what they see and what they think. Remind them the lesson's topic is family.

✏️ **Write:** Have students answer the questions on their own. Review the answers in small groups or with the entire class. Encourage students to freely express their thoughts.

💬 **Comment:** A family is two or more people who have common goals, values, beliefs and traditions, who have long-term commitments to each other and

Understand

Many creatures on Earth form families because they perform important functions that allow them to exist. For humans, the family is the center of our society and a very important building block for strong communities. A family should supply love and care, protection, support, direction, examples, kind words and much more. Each member has a role inside the family. For example, parents give instructions, brothers and sisters share and assist each other, and older family members may share family history and wisdom. One thing is for sure; all family members learn from one another because of the bond between them.

Create - Present your family

Draw, color, cut and paste photos, or use other creative ways to show your family.

In groups of three, compare your families. Write down what you noticed on a sheet of paper. Share your answers with the class.

Reflect

What makes my family special?
How will my family change as I grow up?
What type of family would I like to have in the future?

Willpower

I value my family. They are part of who I am.

---

live together. It is a haven, a secure and safe place to be who you are. It is place of belonging. Family members are bonded be it by blood (biologically) or by heart (emotionally).

 Understand: In some ways, family units are to humanity, what water is to the universe. It is where we originated, where we go back to and what we look for, even if we have had discouraging experiences. Inside the family unit, spoken and unspoken roles and responsibilities exist. It is a structure with unique ties and bonding that are deeply rooted. Describe and discuss the strengths a family structure provides for its members. Encourage students to create their own definition of family. Of course, you will need to be sensitive to students who might not have a family setting, in which you could encourage them to look at the heart ties they have with people around them. You can have students compare the human families with the animal families.

Be sure students understand that just because your family exists does not mean there are no frictions, challenges and problems at times. Those exist in any family unit.

 Create: Students will create a visible presentation of their family, be it a family tree or any other form of art. Encourage them to include all the people they consider family. Help them understand that there is family by blood (physical) and family by heart (emotional.) If time allows, students can write about their families in their journal as a follow-up activity or homework assignment. The writing may include family members' names, roles of each member, and what they feel makes their family special and unique. Have students share and compare their family with one with another.

Here are some questions to guide the students in their writing:
1. Who makes up your family (is it by blood or by heart)? Why do you consider them to be family?
2. What makes each family member special?
3. How is your family similar to other families you know?
4. How is your family different from other families you know?
5. What makes you proud to be a part of your family?

Reflect: Sharing gives them the opportunity to talk about their own experience, but also to recognize the differences between families within a classroom community. This could stimulate students being considerate one of another because more information gives insight.

Willpower

Students should be able to recognize the valuable bonds in their family, (even if there are internal struggles) and that over time, the relationships within the family can change, especially as they develop a greater understanding of family.

Lesson 3

Materials
My Best Me textbook, writing utensils, journal, paper, audiovisual equipment, cloth/bandanna, construction paper, pencil, markers, glue, real or artificial leaves

* Suggestion: You could begin this lesson with the book *Waiting* by Kevin Henkes

Resources
<u>**Student Worksheet:**</u> 4yu.info/?i=98303
<u>**Parent Summary:**</u> 4yu.info/?i=98353
<u>**Video:**</u> How teamwork is dreamwork - 4yu.info/?i=93021

Glossary
bandana, consider, skills, succeed, meerkats, distribute, satisfaction

Motivation
Students might tend to think that doing things by themselves is the best and easiest way to go. However, remind them that starting at birth, they belong to small communities of people.

Working together and cooperating with each other will require the students to develop valuable skills. The benefits and dynamics of working with others are multiple and powerful.

1. There is an increase of shared and individual knowledge as information is exchanged while reaching the objective(s). It stimulates creativity and problem solving. Think of building a campfire; each brings their firewood, a spark ignites the kindling which turns into a blaze.

2. There is a variety of strengths that flow together as each individual contributes to the team's objectives and efforts.

3. Students have a unique opportunity to learn how to trust others and create an environment of safety. Members can open up, be vulnerable and offer help.

4. Sometimes it can cause strife and contention, but learning to deal with these roadblocks will develop character of the individual as well as that of the team.

5. It's likely that a team will take on greater challenges than an individual would, which also increases the chance of personal growth and success.

3 — Together Is Better!

Goal — To learn the value and satisfaction of working with others

Pathways

Game - Let's race!
This game is best done outside or in a hall way. Instructions for a three-legged race:
- Choose a partner.
- Stand with your partner on one side.
- Use a <u>bandanna</u> to tie your right foot to your partner's left foot.
- When your teacher says go, run across the room with your partner.
- Have fun!

Comment
Would you have gone faster by yourself? Why?
What did you need to adjust to be able to run together with your partner? How?
Was it hard to do this activity? Why?

Understand
Let's imagine how life would be if everyone had the same interests and abilities with the same strengths and weaknesses. That would make life pretty boring and it would be impossible to help each other! The best way to work together is to <u>consider</u> others' strengths and <u>skills</u>, and agree on how to work together as a team. Working as a group is a give-and-take process that takes understanding, time and patience. When we participate in a team activity, we notice that each person has their own way of doing things. Sometimes we need to work through our differences in order to <u>succeed</u>.

(14)

Goal
To be able to recognize others' strengths and practice working together in a group setting, discovering, in person, the value of teamwork

Pathways

Game: This is probably best done outside or in a gym. Organize the class into teams of 2 to have a 3-legged race. Encourage students to think together about the race before hand and what challenges they may face.

Comment: Students can individually reply to these questions on their own and then share their answers. Discussing the benefits of communication and how that might effect teamwork. Communication may change the outcome of the race.

Video:
How did the meerkats work together to get the fruit back? Could they have done it on their own? What happens when one meerkat tries to do it alone? 4yu.info/?i=93021

4yu.info/?i=93021

Activity

- Form groups of four and distribute these tasks: 1. Drawer 2. Colorer 3. Gluer 4. Time manager
- You will have 20 minutes to complete this project.
- On a large piece of construction paper, draw a tree and four pieces of fruit.
- Color the tree.
- Glue dry or fresh leaves to the branches.
- Make four pieces of fruit.
- Each person in the group will write their task or responsibility on a piece of fruit.

Reflect

Was the group activity difficult? Why?

What part of the project did I like the most? Why?

What are my abilities and skills? Was I able to use these skills during the project?

Did I help others with their job or could I have helped in other ways? How?

Willpower

When I work with others, we add all of our unique strengths together, giving us all success and satisfaction.

15

Understand: Focus on how teamwork is a give-and-take process and what that really means. What do your students give and what do they receive when they work together with other people. Evaluate with the students other activities where they have had to work together with others. How did that go and what are their thoughts and experiences on those group activities. Discover if your students like working together with other people, and why or why not.

Video: Watch the video of the meerkats and take some time to talk about what they saw that relates to working together. How does this apply to their teamwork efforts.

Activity: It is time to work together. Organize students into groups of 4. They are going to make an artwork together. The textbook suggests a tree, but you can adapt the assignment for your students. If you decide to create the tree, you could take the students outside to find leaves or other objects to add to their artwork and get them physically active. Students can

choose to divide the roles on their own, or they can be given a role. Observe the teams as they are working together. Are members of the groups helping each other? Are they talking to each other? Is each member doing their job? This observation will help in the reflection and class discussion.

Reflect: After the activity, lead a brief discussion using the questions in the student workbook. It might give you an opportunity to evaluate some of the group projects that have happened or prepare the students for group activities that will be taking place.

Encourage students to think about what they would do differently if they played the 3-legged race again.

Willpower

Working together is a great way to accomplish tasks and experience satisfaction because of the connection it creates between individuals with different skills and qualities.

Lesson 4

Materials

My Best Me textbook, writing utensils, journal, paper, audiovisual equipment, construction paper, index cards, markers, crayons and other art supplies
* Suggestion: You can start this lesson by reading *Snotty Crocky* by Carlos Patino.

Resources

Student Worksheet: 4yu.info/?i=98304
Parent Summary: 4yu.info/?i=98354
Video: Why do we make fun of others? - 4yu.info/?i=93031

Glossary

behavior, affect, harsh, encouraging, courteous

Motivation

There is a story about a man talking badly about a neighbor in his town. One day, he repents for his unpleasant behavior and asks the neighbor what he can do to restore the relationship. The neighbor answers him with, "Get a feather pillow, go outside, cut it open and shake the pillow in the wind until it's empty." The man does as he is told and returns to the neighbor wondering if now all is well. The neighbor answers, "Now go and collect the feathers and make the pillow as it was." The man responded, "That is impossible."

This story symbolizes what happens with words; once spoken, they are loose and carried with the wind. Words can be used either as weapons or as gifts. We tend to think that because words are intangible, their impact or damage is minor or insignificant. However, the opposite is true. If you say the word "camel," all your students will immediately have an image in their mind of dromedary because words carry thoughts. We convey our thoughts or put our thoughts in other people's minds with our words, just like saying "camel" puts the thought of a camel in the mind of the hearer. All songs, movies, social media, and advertising implant thoughts in the viewer or listener with words.

It is important to think before we speak, and ask ourselves if the thoughts we are about to send will help or hurt someone.

4 — Words Heal or Hurt

Goal To learn to think before I speak and choose my words with great care

Pathways

Observe

Look at the two different situations:
1. Steven takes his time to answer the questions on his test.
2. Steven takes little or no time to answer his sister.

Comment

Is there a difference in Steven's <u>behavior</u>?
Why does Steven take time to think before he answers the test questions?
Why does Steven answer his sister so quickly?

Understand

Steven thought carefully how to answer the questions on his test because he wanted a good grade. He did not take much time to think about how to answer his sister and how his answer would <u>affect</u> her.

The way we respond and the words we use affect others much more than we can see on the outside. When we speak in a <u>harsh</u> way and use mean words, we harm others and our relationship with them. If we think before we speak, use <u>encouraging</u> words

Goal

To understand the power and impact of words, motivating students to develop the healthy habit of thinking before they speak

Pathways

Observe: Ask the students to describe Steven's behavior in each image. Can they relate to what is happening in those images? Have they behaved in the same manner as Steven, being calm and friendly in one situation and irritated and short in another?

Comment: Use these questions to lead a discussion on the topic and create understanding to the impact words have in our life. In this case, they can help us obtain a good grade or they can hurt

that heal and build others up, and communicate kindly, we help others experience peace and joy in their life as well as in our life. These types of actions usually cause friendly responses.

 Video: 4yu.info/?i=93031

Why do children make fun of other children?

What do you feel when others make fun of you?

Why do you think it hurt Bird when Bernice posted the mean picture of her?

What should Bird do so Bernice stops saying mean things about her?

4yu.info/?i=93031

 Write

What is a friendly way to respond to the following situations?

- A classmate: "I will not let you use my pencils!"

  Me: "_____"

- My mom: "Go clean up your room!"

  Me: "_____"

- A friend: "We will play what I want!"

  Me: "_____"

- A teacher: "Your notebook is a mess!"

  Me: "_____"

 Reflect

What happens when you respond to others in a friendly way?

Do you think before you answer your parents? Your friends?

Is there a difference in how you respond to your friends and parents? Why?

Are you friendly to the strangers that help you (bus driver, cashier, server)?

Willpower

I choose <u>courteous</u> and friendly words when I speak to others.

17

---

on inside of them causing them to react in such ways? How often are people mean because they are hurting or disappointed due to family tension, a recent loss, feeling alone, etc? If students discover the reason for negative and destructive behavior, working towards change might be easier. 4yu.info/?i=93031

Write: Encourage students to be creative in writing down friendly answers to the presented situations. Once they finish, encourage the students to role play the described situations in order to practice using friendly responses in difficult situations. Direct students to switch roles and create their own scenarios. Create time for students to share their answers with each other. It might spike ideas or open up moments of further discussion. The objective is to create more thoughtful behavior in the students in the things they say and do.

Reflect: Follow up with students after they write down their answers and role-play the scenarios. Ask them if they think practicing the strategy of answering in a friendly manner will help them in their future communication with others.

---

someone. If Steven can take time to think about how to answer his test questions, why doesn't he take time to think before he answers his sister?

Understand: Review what was read with your students, and ask them what their thoughts are. The simple act of pausing before speaking can prevent many difficult situations where someone's feelings may get hurt.

Though sometimes students may hurt a person's feelings when they talk, it is never too late for them to learn to practice thinking before speaking. Another way to help students think before they respond is to work with the T-H-I-N-K acronym; (is it True, is it Helpful, is it Inspiring, is it Necessary, is it Kind). You could ask students to create a poster for all to see or index cards for their desk or journal with this acronym to remind them what to do before they react. The THINK concept could become part of your classroom's culture.

Video: There are some questions posted in the textbook tied to this video. Have students investigate their unfriendly or unkind behavior. What really goes

Willpower

Students should understand that what they say and do is always a personal choice. Deciding to stop and think before speaking is a vital habit that will foster healthy relationships with others.

Lesson 5

Materials
My Best Me textbook, writing utensils, journal, paper, audiovisual equipment
* Suggestion: to begin this lesson you could read the book *The Fall of Freddie the Leaf: A Story of Life for All Ages* by Leo Buscaglia.

Resources
Student Worksheet: 4yu.info/?i=98305
Parent Summary: 4yu.info/?i=98355
Video: Considering Others - 4yu.info/?i=93051

Glossary
life cycle, stage, characteristics, phases, mature, infancy, adolescence, purposefully

Motivation
Students will discover that all creatures have a life cycle and go through different developmental stages. Life is a journey. The adjustments we make in each of the different stages help us deal with the different social, cultural, and economical requirements and responsibilities we face. These challenges can be difficult to deal with at the time, which can produce in us the desire to jump to the next life stage.

From the moment of our conception, change and growth is something we will experience on a daily basis. Have students imagine how many cells die off in their body just today (hair, skin, nails, blood, etc.)... about 300 million cells die/minute. Some changes can be challenging and uncomfortable due to the circumstances. However, it is important, that no matter what life stage they are in, students learn to be present in the now and learn to find joy in their environment.

Being respectful and considerate with others in a different life stage is a trait to work on. Students should reflect and consider they have been in the somebody younger life stage and are going to be in that somebody older life stage.

5 Life Stages

Goal To find joy in being who I am at this time in my life

Pathways

Observe
Here is the <u>life cycle</u> of a frog.
Read the names of each <u>stage</u> out loud.

Egg

Tadpole

Adult frog

Young frog or froglet

Tadpole with legs

Comment
What do you notice about the frog's life cycle?
What <u>characteristics</u> do you notice in each stage?
Which stage do you find the most interesting? Why?
Can the frog skip a stage to grow faster? Why or why not?

Understand
Like the frog, all creatures have a life cycle and go through different growing stages. Human beings also go through different <u>phases</u> as they <u>mature</u>: <u>infancy</u>, childhood, <u>adolescence</u>, adulthood, and old age. Each stage follows another and is unique, due to changes in each new stage. Though men and women change in different ways, they all go through the same life stages. It doesn't matter what stage of life we are in, the important thing is to enjoy it!

(18)

Goal

To learn to value, name, and explain the stages of the human life, the unique differences and the joys/ pleasures that come in each of those stages

Pathways

Observe: Invite students to closely study the life cycle of the frog.

Comment: Encourage students to discuss the questions in this section with a partner. Students should realize that skipping stages in life is not an option. To learn to maximize each phase and stage will help their development and advancement.

Understand: Growth and change is a transitioning process for individuals as well as their environment and relationships. As individuals change,

Observe
Look at the image and describe the different characteristics you believe go with each life phase.

Infancy Childhood Adolescence Adulthood Old Age

Game
Can you guess which stage of life I represent? Without telling your classmates which one, act out a stage of the human life cycle. Your classmates will guess which stage you are acting out.

Video: 4yu.info/?i=93051
Watch this video and see how valuable life is no matter which stage you are in. We are who we are because of others who took the time to love us and care for us.

4yu.info/?i=93051

Reflect
What differences are there between a child, an adult, and an elderly person?
Does an individual behave the same way in each different stage of life?
In which stage of life are you? How are you feeling about this stage of your life?
What things can you do as a child that you cannot do when you are an adult?

Willpower

I value all stages of life and purposefully enjoy them all.

19

the people around them change. We tend to forget this aspect of change and growth. A good example is a parent and their child, the needs and care of an infant is far different than that of a teenager. So as the child grows and develops, the parent changes, grows and develops in their parenting role.

In the different phases of life we go through, there are four important processes of development:
1. Mimicry - Babies and children (also when we embark on new things) learn by observing and mimicking those around them in all they do. They follow examples and instructions given (dependent predisposition).
2. Self-discovery - This is when an individual learns what makes him/her different from the rest. This process comes with a lot of trial and error, experimenting on their own, rejecting advice and examples (independent predisposition).
3. Commitment - This is a process in which an individual anchors down and focuses their life on what their strengths and interests are and what helps them advance

in life. They want to maximize their potential and make an impact on the world, leaving a legacy (inter-dependent predisposition).
4. Legacy - This is the process in which an individual maintains the impact and change he/she has brought into the world.

Observe: In the same way students observed the life cycle of a frog early in the lesson, they will now take time to observe the life cycle of a young baby boy as he grows into an elderly man. Maybe they can share what thoughts come to mind as they observe the images of each life phase. The same cycle goes for a female as well.

Game: A students will act out one of the human developmental life stages for the class. Students may use words and props as well as actions to act out the life stage. You can ask students why they think this is the way an individual behaves in that life stage and if the other students would add on to the behavior/words they observed. When the other students guess which life stage is being acted out, have them explain what characteristics make that life cycle unique.

Video: This is an interesting video through which students can get more insight into what happens in the different life stages. A younger adult might feel the pressure of life and the need to stay active, while an older adult, might have more time to enjoy the moment.

Reflect: In small groups, give the students time to think on these questions. Afterward, briefly follow up with students on the thoughts they shared with one another.

Willpower

Being purposeful in valuing and enjoying life in the various stages and respecting others in their life stages will help students experience the greatest benefits for their growth and development.

Identity

Lesson 6

Materials

My Best Me textbook, writing utensils, journal, paper

* Suggestion: A great way to begin this lesson is to read the book *If You Had to Choose* by Sandra McLeod Humphrey.

Resources

Student Worksheet: 4yu.info/?i=98306
Parent Summary: 4yu.info/?i=98356

Glossary

boundaries, respect, internal, hunch, attention, limits, polite, similar, pressure, lack, courage, confident

Motivation

Students do not necessarily know how to discern what is appropriate and what is not when it comes to their behavior. Making wise choices is a skill that develops gradually over time as children mature, and learn from their experiences and from the wisdom they receive from others around them. Students need consistent modeling and support when it comes to learning how to make appropriate choices.

Their inappropriate choices are not necessarily made because students want to suffer. Generally their unwise decisions are made because their (still developing) brain does not emotionally connect consequences to their decisions. If however, they experience some kind of "pain" or loss or they turn a practice into a habit, under discipline (personal or by others) constructive decisions are far more likely to be made.

On this journey of making decisions, students will most likely have to use the word "No" many more times then the word "Yes." For example, inappropriate use of social media and texting, drug and alcohol (ab)use, bullying, nutritional habits, physical exercise and shopping sprees all have to do with potential choices. Students can either say "Yes" or "No."

6 — I Know When to Say "NO"

Goal — To learn that saying "no" can be the right way to take care of myself

Pathways

Read "Nela and the Cake"

One day, Nela's aunt baked a cake for her. It looked delicious. Nela sat down and enjoyed a giant piece of cake that her aunt had cut for her. When she finished, her aunt said, "Here, have another piece." Nela was already full, but she did not want to say "no" to her aunt, so she took the cake and began to eat it. After eating half of her second piece of cake, Nela felt like she could not eat anymore. Her aunt said, "Don't waste the delicious cake that I made for you. Why don't you finish that piece?" So Nela finished the piece of cake. After finishing the cake, Nela felt very sick. She ate too much cake! Now she was too full and had a stomach ache.

Comment

What happened to Nela?
Why was her stomach hurting?
Could Nela have avoided feeling sick? How?

Understand

Often we accept invitations to participate in things that could be harmful to us. That is what happened to Nela. Clear limits or boundaries help us to respect and care for ourselves.

20

Goal

To understand that when wise and positive choices, are made, with confidence and respect, the word "No" will far more often need to be used than "Yes"

Pathways

 Read: Students can read the short story by themselves or with a partner.

 **Comment:** Students should connect the consequences Nela suffered (stomach ache, being upset with her aunt, possible future dislike of cake) with the choice she made. For additional connection, encourage students to brainstorm situations in which they did not say "No" and what consequences they experienced. (This could also happen in small groups.) How come they did not say "No" in each of the

There are moments when we have an internal voice or a "hunch" that tells us to not do or accept something someone offers us. It is important to pay attention to that inner voice. When we want to set limits, it should be enough to say, "No, thank you." However, if our answer is not accepted by the other person, then we can, in a polite way, walk away from the situation.

 Observe

"Come on, let's go to my house!"

Classroom 7

"Stay and talk to us for a while, the teacher isn't here yet."

Reflect

What would I do in a similar situation?

What emotion do I sense when I know I should say "no" but I do not do so?

Do I know my limits? An example of a limit in my life is...

_____

Am I brave enough to firmly say "no" and stick with it, especially in difficult situations where I feel pressure? Please explain.

What do I do if I lack the courage to say "no"?

Willpower

I care for myself by knowing when and how to say "no" in a confident and kind manner.

21

circumstances they presented. Avoid students judging, criticizing or making fun of each other. Allow students to advise each other on how they could have dealt with the situation in a different manner, and what kind of results that would have produced. Invite students to act out their scenarios to give them opportunities to practice saying "No" in a confident, firm and friendly manner.

Understand: A student can read this sections while the other students quietly follow along. Invite students to share their thoughts. Help students understand why it seems so hard to say "No" at times and what they can do to strengthen their ability to say "No" in a firm but polite manner.

Here are some quotes, to increase students' insight on how successful people have viewed saying "No."

Steve Jobs: "Focusing is about saying no."

Warren Buffett: "We need to learn the slow 'yes' and the quick 'no'."

Tony Blair: "The art of leadership is saying no, not saying yes. It is very easy to say yes."

Observe: In the two scenarios presented, the boy and the girl are in a dilemma as to what choice they need to make. Have students reflect on what these children are facing, their choices, and the consequences tied to those choices. Again, ask your students if they have found themselves in similar circumstances and what happened in their situation. Also, see if they will share what they experienced emotionally in those situations.

Make a list on the white board of as many common situations where "no" is the wise answer. Flip the situation and ask them what could or did happen if they used the word "Yes" in those situations. Give students time to think it through and guide their critical thinking with questions so they understand how choices have consequences.

Reflect: Allow students to write or discuss the questions addressed in this section based on their observations. Remind students that there are no right or wrong answers to these questions. They are tools to stimulate their thinking and increase their insight.

End the lesson by an occurrence in their own lives in which they confidently said "No" and how that make them feel.

Willpower

Students will have developed more confidence on how to make decisions that will protect them and others. Encourage them to create a habit out of saying "No" more often than "Yes."

Lesson 7

Materials

My Best Me textbook, writing utensils, journal, paper, modeling clay for each student, crayons, markers or colored pencils

* Suggestions: The book *Humble Pie* by Jennifer Donnelly and the story "The Emperor's New Clothes" by Hans Christian Andersen could be used to begin the lessons.

Resources

Student Worksheet: 4yu.info/?i=98307
Parent Summary: 4yu.info/?i=98357

Glossary

recognize, humble, mold, carved, sculpted, attitude, modest, morals, flexible

Motivation

Students should realize that many people influence their lives, molding and shaping them into who they are. If students begin each day with a humble attitude, ready to listen and learn from others through revelation instead of personal experience (the school of hard-knocks) they open the door to growth and new opportunities. The word "humble" may be a new concept for some students. The following link can be helpful to read before exploring the topic with your students. 4yu.info/?i=93071

Students should learn to appreciate the advice they receive from parents, teachers, coaches, classmates, and realize that being open to the suggestions of others will positively impact their growth and development. Sound advice can give them insight and revelation on how to avoid negative and destructive consequences.

As the adults in the lives of students and children, we might need to be more open to hearing what these youngsters have to say or what they might hand us. Many times, they are trying to tell us something, but, often, we tend to be too busy to hear them and appreciate their contribution.

7 Upward Every Day

Goal

To <u>recognize</u> that I can learn from others

Pathways

💬 **Comment**
What does the word "<u>humble</u>" mean?

✏️ **Create**
Use modeling clay to create a tree in 10 minutes.

💬 **Comment**
Were you able to finish creating the tree during the time allowed? How did your tree turn out? Was it easy to <u>mold</u> the clay? Why? What would you have experienced if you had <u>carved</u> it out of wood? What would you have experienced if you had sculpted a tree out of a rock?

💡 **Understand**
During our life, we are formed and shaped by the people and situations around us. However, that process of formation can be easily done like the molding of a lump of clay, or difficult like the carving of a piece of wood, or the sculpting of a stone. Just like the tree, we are either molded, carved or <u>sculpted</u> by the people around us who play a part in our growth. Our <u>attitude</u> decides how we are going to be developed and taught by others. The key is to have a humble and <u>modest</u> attitude (not negative or bossy), yet strong enough to stand up for our values and <u>morals</u>. A humble and

(22)

Goal

To recognize that being a humble and flexible learner will create opportunities for accelerated growth and development, and helps avoid harsh consequences

Pathways

✏️ **Create:** Mold it! Explain to the students that they have 10 minutes to create a tree with modeling clay. They can mold any tree they like. While they are working, ask them the questions in the book and expound on their answers.

💬 **Comment:** Is the clay easy to mold and shape? What aspect of the clay makes it easy to use for sculpting? What skills did it require?

Once the students are finished, have them form groups of 3 or 4 and show their trees. Ask students to

modest person is someone who is:

1. Aware that he/she needs help and can ask for it boldly
2. Focused on other people
3. Helpful, kind and responsible in all he/she does
4. Led by morals and values
5. Thankful and grateful even in difficult situations
6. Open to receiving instructions and corrections
7. Ready to admit his/her mistakes and is willing to ask forgiveness.

Think about a humble and modest person you know. Are there other ways to describe them? What are they?

_____ _____ _____ _____

 Observe

Look at the first image. How would you react? Circle one of the last two images.

 Reflect

Describe the image you circled.
Why did you pick that image?
What is the best way to respond to the instructions of your teachers, parents or caregivers?
Why is it healthier for you to be flexible and open to new ideas?

 Willpower

I am <u>flexible</u> and listen to what others say, so I can learn from them.

23

---

thoughtfully critique the trees, sharing how they could improve their tree. Motivate students to take the advice they received and give them time to adjust or correct their trees.

In addition to the concept of flexibility, this activity ties directly into the notion of being humble, as students react to their classmates' observations on the tree they have created. Ask students how they felt about other students "critiquing" them. Here are examples of some question you could ask:

- Was it hard to show your tree to your classmates?
- What did you think about the observations you received from your classmates?
- Did you take their advice and work more on your tree?
- Did their observations hurt you or did it motivate you to improve your efforts?
- How did your classmates react to your observations on their efforts?
- Was it difficult to be truthful and yet friendly while giving the observations?
- Did anyone in your group change their tree after the

observations were given?

In an abstract manner, these questions relate to being flexible and learning from others. It may be difficult for some students to understand, so encourage a class discussion to help make this connection more concrete.

Understand: Focus on the descriptions of the word "humble." Allow students to give their opinion concerning these descriptions and be sure they comprehend their significance. Have a class discussion about what it means to be "humble." Elicit examples of how to show humility.

It is difficult to be around people who are not humble or who think they already know everything. When things go wrong, such people tend to blame others because they take on the role of the victim. Every healthy relationship is based on giving and receiving, so if someone claims to have nothing to learn from the other person, the giving aspect of that relationship is lost. The person who is trying to help/teach will not feel like they can contribute to the relationship, which is likely to cause tension.

Observe: Have students observe the images and ask them what they think is going on. Ask them if something similar might have happened with them. Allow students to share. The students should mark the decision that they would make in the pictured situation.

Reflect: Allow students to write or respond to the questions in the workbook. Remind the students that not all questions have a right or wrong answer.

Willpower

When students understand the value of being humble and flexible and are willing to listen and learn from others with an open mind, they will decrease the pressure on their life of trying to live up to other people's expectation.

Lesson 8

Materials

My Best Me textbook, writing utensils, journal, paper, markers or colored pencils paper, paper bag, small folded pieces of paper, audiovisual equipment
* Suggestion: A great way to begin this lesson is to read the book *Sir Morgan and the Kingdom of Horrible Food* by Candice Cameron and Isabella Inwalle.

Resources

Student Worksheet: 4yu.info/?i=98308
Parent Summary: 4yu.info/?i=98358
Food Pyramid: 4yu.info/?i=93081
Food Chart: 4yu.info/?i=98431

Glossary

influence, well-being, stung, affect, damaging, consequences, menu, conversation, balanced, improve

Motivation

It is a human tendency to blame others for our problems, but the truth is that we each make our own choices. Students should understand this at young age. Therefore, it is not too soon to teach third graders about making healthy choices. Moreover, that their choices affect their overall well-being; both in the short and long term. Making healthy choices becomes easier when we turn the practice into a habit. This insight will make children become more independent, responsible, and confident.

You can start a simple yet effective habit. Ask the students to keep track of all the things they eat and drink, the quantity and the time they do so, for one day each week. Attached is a simple template that you can copy or print out for your students to keep track. (Here is the link: Book 3 Lesson 8 Chart.) 4yu.info/?i=98431

Suggest accountability groups as they develop this habit and share what they have written down and what they are thinking (journaling). In the book *The Power of Habits*, Charles Duhigg explains the great success available in habitually journaling to bring about change in many daily habits.

8 My Health Begins with Me

 Goal   To understand that my choices greatly influence my overall health and well-being

Pathways

Game

- Choose a piece of paper from a bag.
- Look at your piece of paper: if it has the name of a bug, call it out.
- The person who is "the bug" will try to "sting" the others by tagging them.
- If the "bug" classmate touches other classmates, they will act as if they are stung and sit down. They are "out."
- When all players have been "stung," the game is over and a new round can start, using a different "bug."

Comment

What did you do when the "bug" person was near?
In life, what measures do you take to avoid being "stung" by sickness or disease?
Who's decisions have the greatest affect on your health? Please explain.

Understand

In the game, if a player ran away, he or she did not get stung. To get stung by a bug would mean you lost and would be out of the game. This is what happens in life: when we are "stung" with sickness it keeps us from being involved in all of the activities that we enjoy and cuts us off from other people.

 **Goal**

To understand that making healthy choices is a personal responsibility, and that doing so on a consistent basis will result in developing healthy life-long habits

 **Pathways**

Game: Bring the students outside, a gym or to an area where there is room to run around. They will play a game that can enhance their understanding of how infections can spread if we do not take the right precautions. Beforehand, prepare slips of paper to the count of your students and put them in a bag. All of the folded slips of paper will remain blank with the exception of one, which will have the name of a stinging insect listed on it. Prepare more slips of paper with the names of other bugs or insects on them to switch out with each new game.

The decisions we make each day play a role in whether or not we have a cheerful or gloomy attitude. For example, we choose what, when, and how much to eat. We choose when and how we rest, who to hang out with, what we believe, and what we do in our free time. If the decisions we make are damaging, we will experience the consequences. However, if we take responsibility for our decisions and want to care for our health, we will make positive choices, seeing positive results as we grow.

Create a **Menu**

Let's focus on our food decisions. Few things affect us faster than the foods we decide to eat. Use a food pyramid (link: flives.us/?i=93081) and with a partner ...

- Think about your favorite meal and create a menu describing the food in that meal.
- After you have created your menu, share it with a partner.
- When talking with your partner, share the reasons for your choices. Use the questions below to guide your conversation.

Reflect

Did you and your partner create complete, balanced, and satisfying meal? Is the meal healthy? Please explain.

What would be an unhealthy meal? Give at least one example.

What would happen if you ate an unhealthy dinner every night?

How do you feel when you eat a healthy meal?

How do you feel when you eat an unhealthy meal?

What are some of the long-term effects of eating poorly?

What other constructive aspects are related to food?

 **Willpower**

I am responsible for my health and will improve my meal choices.

27

The directions are as follows:
- Invite students to pull one slip of paper from the bag.
- The student with the name of "the bug" on the slip will call it out.
- The "bug" student will try to sting others by tagging them
- The other students can avoid getting stung by running away. (You can expand the game by having students hide or creating safe zones)
- Anyone touched by the "bug" will act as if they are in pain and will sit down.
- Once all players are stung you can play the game again using a different bug name.

Comment: Evaluate the game with the students and keep relating to what happens to them in life when their choices could result in them not being able to participate because they were taken out of the game due to lack of sleep, unhealthy diet, eating disorders, lack of activity or exercise, drugs, alcohol and much more.

Understand: We want the students to develop the idea that they are, in large part, in control of their own health. They have far more influence on their own health than they probably imagined. As they evaluate some of their health choices they might come to realize that they need to make some changes to their lifestyle. However, for them to be successful in establishing new healthy habits, they will need to know that this is a step by step process. Therefore, this lesson focuses mostly on them getting insight and understanding into their eating habits. We want to encourage them to start making healthy decisions on what they eat, when they eat and how they eat their meals.

Create: Students will create a dinner menu for their family. Beforehand, encourage students to think about the many courses a dinner may contain. Brainstorm as a class and make a list on the board of the different courses of a meal (salad, soup, appetizer, main course, dessert, etc.). Also, invite them to think about what they would enjoy eating for dinner compared to what they regularly eat at home. How are these foods the same or different?

If time allows, set up a class restaurant where the students can practice ordering healthy foods. They could work as a group to develop one group menu, a name, and sign for the restaurant, etc.

Reflect: Use the questions to discuss the created menus. Students may reflect on the lesson in verbal or written format.

Willpower

It is important to understand that short and long term choices on the food and drinks the students consume, how, when, and even with whom they consume them can affect their health, positively or negatively.

Lesson 9

Materials
My Best Me textbook, writing utensils, journal, paper, markers, colored pencils, square pieces of colored paper, colored sticky notes, poster board, glue, tape, stickers, magazine clippings, scissors, photo of each student
* Suggestion: A great book to read with this lesson is *Healthy Choices, Happy Kids: Making Good Choices with Everyday Care* by Foster W. Cline, Lisa C. Greene, and Gina L. May.

Resources
Student Worksheet: 4yu.info/?i=98309
Parent Summary: 4yu.info/?i=98359

Glossary
enthusiasm, complex, emotions, environment, invention, design, relationships, volunteer, compliments, encourage, affection, forgiving, review, decorate

Motivation
Being healthy means so much more than just eating a balanced diet and getting some exercise. Help your students understand that health means that there is order, harmony and balance between all aspects of their being (mind, soul, spirit and body) in relationship to their environment. Health has to do with embracing life (the positive and negative) and using it to advance and grow strong and be resilient.

Forming constructive and powerful habits to maintain our health in all aspects of our existence does not come naturally to us. Some habits we learn from family members, while others may require a constant effort of discipline to put them into practice. Living unhealthy is easier, cheaper, more fun, but it always comes with a consequence, which is usually negative.

As third-graders learn to develop this mindset of taking responsibility for their own health, they will increase their chance at living a life of satisfaction and purpose.

9 The Kaleidoscope of Health

Goal To learn that my health is related to many different areas of my life

Pathways

Understand
When we are healthy, we can live our lives with energy and enthusiasm. Though this sounds easy, the truth is that health is a complex issue that has to do with many areas of life including our bodies, our minds, our emotions, our schools and our environment. All these areas are knit together with the daily choices we make, and they all play a role in how we feel and how we experience life.

Draw - On the following lists, circle the healthy things you do each day.
With my body: Keep myself clean, drink at least 8 glasses of water, eat a balanced diet, sleep at least 8 hours, play outside, exercise.
With my mind: Do my school work, read books, play games, do puzzles, draw, learn to play an instrument, sing, create an invention, cook, build, design.
With my relationships with others: Obey my parents and teachers, spend time with my friends, visit family, volunteer in my community, share my things, help others, give compliments, encourage others, show my affection, give gifts, greet those around me, say "please" and "thank you."
With my inner self: Be thankful, be forgiving, listen to good music, sit alone and think, be caring, make wise decisions, help others, be honest, be nice to someone who is not friendly, journal, take a stand for what I believe in.

Comment
Review the activities you did not mark.

(28)

Goal

To help your students understand that their health is related to many different aspects of their life, and to practice making healthy choices in all these areas

Pathways

Understand: Make sure your students understand what a kaleidoscope is and how it would relate to health. Explain to students that on a daily basis they make many choices that affect them physically, mentally, emotionally, socially, spiritually, and financially. These different facets of their existence are like the sections in a kaleidoscope; all the decisions they make are like the beads and sparkles, constantly on the move. As life slowly turns, different impressions and conditions are reflected; sometimes the experience is beautiful and lively, while other times it might be dull and gloomy. The

Do you think these activities are healthy? Why or why not?

Which activities do you plan to add to your daily life? Why?

What other healthy things do you do that are not on the list?

Game

- Form a circle with your classmates. The teacher will tell you where to go.
- Your teacher will start the game and will name something healthy.
- The next student in line will use the last letter of that word and mention another healthy thing until the last student shares. For example: If the teacher says "vegetables" the next student will use the letter S and may say "sleep," and then the next one uses the P for "play," etc.

Create

Make a poster about you! Gather different colored square pieces of paper. On each piece of paper write a word that has to do with healthy activities that you do. Write down one <u>detailed</u> action with each word. For example Water: 8 glasses/day. In the middle of a large piece of poster paper, glue a picture of yourself. Around your picture, glue the written words. See the example. <u>Decorate</u> your poster to emphasize how healthy you are.

Rest · Family · Diet · Hygiene · Photo · Excercises · Affection · Water · Friends

Reflect

The poster project will remind you that you are responsible for your health. Hang this on the wall of your bedroom, the refrigerator, or in the classroom to help you reflect on your daily decisions and habits.

Willpower

I live with purpose! I develop healthy habits for my life!

---

intent is to help students to become aware of and analyze some of the choices they make and how these decisions and actions affect their health.

Draw: To gain insight on the complexity of health, have them circle the healthy actions that they take each day. There are no right or wrong answers. The activity is merely an invitation to evaluate and consider the choices they make concerning their well-being. Encourage students to add to these lists any other activities they undertake on a daily basis that affect their health that might not be mentioned.

Comment: Have students discuss their responses to the activity as well as the questions presented in this sections, with a partner, in a small group, or as a class. Students can discover how their peers make decisions and what kind of choices they make. Sharing their answers and thoughts with each other may reveal to them an area of improvement or a cultural difference to be recognized and celebrated.

Game: This is a Word Chain game. Give students time to answer as they participate. Form a circle around the room, start the game and name something healthy. The student to the right will build on what was said using the last letter of the word mentioned. That letter will become the first letter of the healthy thing they mention. Have this word chain continue until the last student shares their health insight. For example: If you say "vegetables," the next student may say "sleep," and then the next one might say "play," etc. If you think it might help their learning process to write the words down or make the game more dynamic, you could use the white board. An option is to then invite each student to write down their word when it is their turn.

Create: Use colored sticky notes or have students cut small squares of colored paper, about 10-12 squares. The objective is to create a health poster that reflects ways the student chooses to maintain a healthy lifestyle. They need a picture of themselves and then words/activities related to health. Students will need to detail the word or activity they use. For example, "Rest: I sleep 8 hours every night." If you prefer, assign students to cut out images from magazines or print images at home that mean something healthy to them.

Reflect: Encourage students to think about the many facets of health, questioning why they do certain activities and why they don't do other ones. The simple fact that they consider their actions and talk about it with their peers will increase their awareness of how important their decisions are in relationship to their health.

Willpower

The greatest place to begin purposeful living is with the subject of health. Increasing students' understanding and insight will result in them developing habits that increase their overall well-being.

Lesson 10

Materials
My Best Me textbook, writing utensils, journal, paper, markers, colored pencils, audiovisual equipment, construction paper, index cards

* Suggestion: A great way to begin this lesson is to read the book *I Think I Am* by Louise L. Hay and Kristina Tracy.

Resources
Student Worksheet: 4yu.info/?i=98310
Parent Summary: 4yu.info/?i=98360
Video: *Have You Filled A Bucket Today?* - 4yu.info/?i=93091
Articles: 4yu.info/?i=93092
4yu.info/?i=93093

Glossary
content, generous, pleasant, sorry

Motivation
Being healthy implies being whole and being in order. It requires daily discipline. If we desire a long and healthy life, our invisible (inside) self as well as our visible (outside) self needs continuous, care and attention.

If we are going to focus on a healthy mind, students need insight on how their mind is shaped. You have probably heard this saying: "Follow your gut, listen to your heart and use your head." Why? Because our head, heart and gut all have brain cells that collect data and form how and what we think. Attached are two videos that will give you more insight. 4yu.info/?i=93092, 4yu.info/?i=93093

Creating and maintaining a strong, clean and focused mind has to do with what we allow ourselves to be exposed to. Our mind is especially formed by what we see and hear. If students expose themselves to positive, caring influences, those images and sounds will "program" their brains and create a healthy, orderly mind. If students expose themselves to negative, destructive influences, those images and sounds will "program" their brains and create an unhealthy, disorderly mind. Each person behaves according to their "programming."

10 Clean Mind, Content Life

Goal To learn that taking care of how I feel on the inside is as important as taking care of the outside

Pathways

💬 **Comment**

What makes you happy? Write down five things that make you happy. (It could be a favorite place, an activity, a person, etc.)

1. _____
2. _____
3. _____
4. _____
5. _____

Compare your list with your classmates. Did any of you have the same ideas?

💡 **Understand**

We clean our bodies regularly in order to stay healthy. Did you know that it is just as important to keep our thoughts and feelings "clean?" We will thrive in every area of our lives when we keep our minds at peace, our hearts content, we are generous and pleasant with friends, and always have something positive to say to others.

Sometimes, things happen that make us feel sad or angry, or we can say words or do things that hurt someone's feelings, maybe without realizing it. These situations can turn into more serious problems if they are not quickly handled. Talking about the way you feel and why you feel that way can help keep your mind and heart "clean." Telling someone that you are sorry for hurting them and asking for forgiveness are two ways to care for yourself. How do you feel when you say sorry? How do you feel when someone says sorry to you?

Goal

To create insight that good mental hygiene can only exist by shielding and protecting ourselves against visual and audible negative (violence, cursing, abuse, etc.) influences

Pathways

💬 **Comment:** Begin the lesson with students reflecting on what makes them happy. Allow them to compare their thoughts with their classmates. Be sure to take a look at what students write down.

💡 **Understand:** Have students think about a strong, stable and healthy mind. What does that look like? What will they need to do to create and maintain a healthy mind? (Make a comparison to how we care for our bodies: diet-what we consume; exercise-what activities and training we do; hygiene-what do we do to

Video: 4yu.info/?i=93091
Watch, "Have You Filled A Bucket Today?"

4yu.info/?i=93091

 Apply

Create a small bucket out of a sheet of paper. Write a positive note to a classmate and place it in their bucket. Read some of the notes as a class, or post them on the bulletin board.

 Create

Make a series of index cards titled "I Feel Healthy on the Inside." On each card, draw a picture, write some words, paste photos, and/or pictures that describe what makes your mind and heart feel healthy. You may list actions, such as saying "sorry" if you hurt someone, reading books, listening to music, thinking of a person who has had a positive impact on your life, writing out your thoughts and dreams, etc.

After sharing your cards with some classmates, take them home and place them somewhere as a daily reminder of the choices you can make to guard your mind and heart from negative influences. It will help you remember that staying healthy involves more than just brushing your teeth and washing your hands.

 Reflect

What can I do today to feel healthy on the inside?

_____

_____

Willpower

I choose to be grateful and keep my mind and heart clean, so I can be healthy on the inside as well as on the outside.

31

---

clean and refresh ourselves; sleep/rest-what do we do to restore and settle down).

Some major steps students can take to mind their mind: They need to learn how to guard themselves against negative and destructive influences. They are responsible to put limits and defenses up against what information they allow into their thinking patterns (through their eyes and ears). They need to discover how to replace negative thoughts with uplifting, constructive, and edifying thoughts. They need to review their relationships and free themselves of toxic friends and connections. They need to learn to develop a positive outlook on the world and focus on others, caring for people around them.

Video: 4yu.info/?i=93091 This story is to help students immediately put into action something that will improve their mind. Have students make their own paper buckets by folding paper into squares with a bottom. The students can be creative in creating their bucket. Students will learn to become "bucket fillers," writing

---

compliments and encouraging notes to one another.

Create: Students will make inspirational index cards "I Feel Happy on the Inside" to train their brains to think positively. The cards can include words, photos, pictures and decorations that describe what makes them feel happy and content. They may list actions, such as forgiving another person, volunteering their time to help others, etc. They can reference books, songs, or movies that have influenced them, a person who has had a positive impact on their life, or write out their thoughts and dreams. Encourage them to use these cards to keep them on track, especially when they are not feeling their best.

The purpose of these activities is for students to learn how easily they can switch from a negative, downcast mindset to a positive, uplifting mindset. They decide!

After the game, give students the chance to reflect on how maintaining a strong mind by creating positive thoughts can foster a happier state of well-being. Students may respond with a partner, small group, or in written form, or you can write some of their happy words on a board. As a result, students will gain a broader understanding of the wide variety of things that make people feel happy; some they will have in common, some they will not relate to.

Reflect: Students will commit to at least one action that they will take that day to help them feel happier on the inside. Do a follow-up at the beginning of the next class to discuss their experiences.

Willpower

Students will realize that they are the key to keeping their mind healthy by managing the thought processes they have and by what they allow themselves to be exposed to.

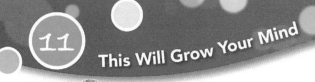

Materials
My Best Me textbook, writing utensils, journal, paper, audiovisual equipment

Resources
Student Worksheet: 4yu.info/?i=98311
Parent Summary: 4yu.info/?i=98361
Video: Meet Brick Brain - 4yu.info/?i=93101

Glossary
Fixed Mindset, Growth Mindset, optimistic, challenges, talent, mini workshop, participant, statement,

Motivation
For years, scientists thought that a person was born with a certain amount of intelligence and ability; that the brain was "fixed" or "programmed" and could not be changed. Dr. Carol Dweck decided to challenge that thought 30 years ago, believing that the brain actually can develop and that we can improve our intelligence.

The problem is, our society for a greater part still believes that the brain is a fixed entity; that our talents, gifts, and intelligence are "set in stone," and there's nothing we can do to change that. That is false. We will see in this lesson that scientists are proving that the brain can adapt, grow and change. This is the difference between a Growth Mindset and a Fixed Mindset.

Students will understand that the only limits to their brain potential are the limits they place on it. The brain is, truly, an amazing organ. Though scientists have been studying it ardently for hundreds of years, and neuroscience has made significant discoveries, the brain is still an unexplored universe of possibilities. If your students can walk away from this lesson with just one truth, it should be that the brain is flexible or "elastic," and if you put your mind to something, you can achieve it.

Goal To learn that I have the power to make myself smarter

Pathways

Understand
Did you know that you can make yourself smarter? Our brains act like muscles; they get stronger with more use. Challenging our brain to do something, makes it sharp. Dr. Carol Dweck discovered that the only thing that limits our brain is when we say, "I can't." We should always choose to use the words, "I can do this." If we study, practice and stretch our brains, we will become smarter. We should decide to never give up on anything we want to do or learn.

A Growth Mindset is when we believe that our brain is able to learn and do anything we tell it to do. A Fixed Mindset is when a person believes that they are limited in how smart they can be.

A person with a Fixed Mindset believes that if they fail in a certain task, they will always fail in that task. A person with a Growth Mindset believes that with a lot of practice and an optimistic attitude, they can improve and get better at any task. They "believe in the power of yet." Let's listen to the book below to learn about "the power of yet" as Julia Cook explains what Dr. Dweck is talking about.

Video: 4yu.info/?i=93101
Take a moment to look at this clip

Comment
What were some challenges Brick Brain faced?

4yu.info/?i=93101

32

Goal
To discover how to make yourself smarter by adopting a Growth Mindset and how that is key to enhancing the learning process in every area of life

Pathways

Understand: Students should understand that the brain is the most complex organ in our body and it consumes one third of our energy intake. Every year, science makes new, amazing discoveries about the power and potential of the brain.

If you can help your third graders grasp the Growth Mindset concept, you will be setting them up for a paradigm shift in their thinking! The truth about the brain is that its performance abilities are unlimited. We are not destined to be bad at math, science or sports for the rest of our lives. It truly is about the desire of our heart; if we

Did Bubble Gum Brain treat challenges differently?

Have you ever behaved like Brick Brain? Please explain.

Have you behaved like Bubble Gum Brain? Please explain.

What was the most important thing Brick Brain learned at the end of the story?

 Activity

What is your talent? Singing? Basketball? Drawing? Or are you well informed about a certain subject that interests you? Share that talent and/or information with your classmates by holding a "mini workshop" in class, teaching others your skill, talent or knowledge. The class will form groups small enough so every participant can learn and practice something new. Be sure to join a group that is teaching something you do not know, not know how to do or cannot do well... yet! Take time each week to attend your mini workshop.

 Write

Create a "not yet, but I will" statement (e.g., "I don't know how to .... yet, but I will practice .... daily to learn this new skill).

_____

_____

Reflect

Was it difficult to develop a "not yet" statement? Practice this "not yet" statement for 63 days and then come back to the classroom and tell everyone about your experience of using your Growth Mindset.

Repeat after me:
"I Can do This"

Willpower

If I believe I can, I will. I believe I can always learn something new, so I will become smarter.

---

put our willpower to work, apply ourselves and diligently and with discipline work hard, we will improve in any area where we previously believed we couldn't.

Does it mean that if we are terrible at basketball, we can still become the next NBA superstar? Not necessarily, but we will get better at basketball. Help your students understand that their brain can take them further than they ever thought possible!

Video: 4yu.info/?i=93101 - Watch and read the book Bubble Gum Brain. Engage the class in questions about the video. The goal is to help your students grasp the concept of a Growth Mindset versus a Fixed Mindset, and that each of them have unlimited learning and growing potential in every area.

Activity: Set up mini workshops with volunteer students leading each 3-4 member workshop. The leader of the workshop will be teaching other students a talent or skill that the leader possesses and that the other students want to learn. Keep this simple: ask for volunteers who can lead a mini workshop on such skills

as dance, shooting a basketball, playing an instrument (such as guitar), art skills, etc. Make sure that every student finds a workshop, and if you have students who have a hard time choosing a group, prompt them with a question such as, "Have you ever dreamed of being a musician, actor, scientist, or athlete? From there, you can direct them to an appropriate workshop.

Comment: Talk through the concept of "The Power of Yet" with your class. They may not "yet" be good at the hula hoop, but with practice, they can learn and will be. Ask students to share one "yet" goal with the class. For example, "I am not yet great at math, but I will ask for help and practice until I am." After this exercise, reassure your students that if one way doesn't work to solve a math problem (or another area of presumed weakness), then we try another way until we get it right. Our brains are not like cement that cannot be formed into something else once it has dried. Our brains are like silly putty; elastic and flexible!

Write: Make sure each student writes out a "not yet, but I will" statement that addresses an area they want to learn. If they need help, buddy them up with another classmate.

Reflect: Prompt students to share their statement. Encourage them to declare their statement aloud for 63 days. You may want to check in with your students on their "not yet" exercise. Talk briefly about how their statements and attitude are changing their way of thinking about their potential and abilities.

Willpower

Have students realize that their brain is like muscle; the more they work it, the stronger it gets! Stretching the brain creates powerful connections. Doing difficult things is a useful exercise that students need to try, and if need be, try again until they succeed.

Lesson 12

Materials
My Best Me textbook, writing utensils, journal, paper, 2 different colored balloons for each pair of students, markers, colored pencils, crayons

* You may want to just use two balloons for the whole class, and you blow up the balloons. If available, use little hand pumps.

* Suggestion: A great book to read is the "Jolly Time Book" series title called *That Stinks: Find Your Dream World in the Beautiful Outdoors* by Karen S. McGowan and Dennis E. McGowan.

Resources
Student Worksheet: 4yu.info/?i=98312
Parent Summary: 4yu.info/?i=98362
Articles: Here are 12 benefits of being outdoors - 4yu.info/?i=93111

Glossary
inflate, deflate, appears, condition, surroundings, wear, strained, routine, imaginative, explore,

Motivation
Being outside is a refreshing and healthy habit students should develop and maintain throughout their life. With all of the demands of school, work, and everyday life, most families do not go outdoors as often as they should. At the same time, social media is aggressively encroaching on the time management of most people in society. Teach children the importance of physical activity and outdoor recreation. The more a child experiences how much fun it is to relax, play outside, and just "be," the more likely they will choose outdoor activities.

You might want to create a small group of students to help plan outdoor activities for the class each day. You can change the group members each week, or request volunteers. Consider outings that are separate from their snack or lunch breaks, and that are tied to the learning taking place in their classes. Plan activities that bring to life the subject matter you are teaching, allowing students to discover the true joy and value of spending time in nature. Take into consideration any weather changes and prepare for them accordingly.

12 Outside Fun

 Goal

To understand the health benefit of being active outdoors.

 Pathways

Activity
Select a partner and complete the following steps:

Step 1
- Inflate a balloon and deflate it.
- Repeat this same action five times.
- Observe the characteristics of this balloon and write down your findings.

Step 2
- Inflate another balloon and tie off the end.
- Observe its characteristics and write down your observations.
- Play with the balloon for 5 minutes with your partner.

 Comment
How did the balloon that was inflated and deflated 5 times look and feel?
How did the balloon that was inflated just once look and feel?
What balloon appears to be in better condition at the end of the activity? Why?
What is the purpose of balloons?

 Understand
Balloons are made for having fun and decorating our surroundings. When we inflate and deflate a balloon time after time, we are not using it in the way it was meant to be used. We wear out the balloon by inflating and deflating it.

34

Goal

To learn the great benefits there are in doing outdoor activities, adventures, and relaxation on a daily basis, appreciate and enjoy it

Pathways

Activity: This activity will require a decent amount of space. Feel free to go outside to play, or move desks to allow ample space. The first phase is to show students what happens to a balloon when you blow it up, and empty it out, blow it up and empty it out. It stretches and weakens the balloon. The purpose of the activity is to show students that when we get caught up in our daily routines, we may forget to allow enough time for rest, relaxation, and fun experiences outdoors, and just like the balloon, we wear thin, our muscles become

How do you feel when you do the same activity over and over again? For example, do you like watching the same TV show for many hours, or sitting in the same spot for a long time? Could we feel stretched and strained doing the same thing many times over? Just like the balloon needs to be used properly, our bodies need proper exercise and outdoor time.

We can change our routine by the simple decision to go outside daily; to play in the fresh air, planning new and imaginative adventures and trips. These actions will give us fresh energy and help us feel strong and healthy. There is a new world to explore every day! We will benefit more from life when we whole-heartedly decide to enjoy each moment, each corner of our planet and every beautiful creature in nature. This will help us take care of our bodies, both inside and out.

Draw
Create a picture of your favorite outdoor place.

Reflect
How many times a week do you go outside to enjoy outdoor life?
How many hours do you spend sitting inside on a couch, bed, or chair?
How many of those hours inside are you in front of a screen?
What are your favorite outdoor activities?
Is there a new place you'd like to explore that is outside?

Willpower
I spend time outside to refresh myself and keep myself healthy.

35

flaccid, we loose directions and purpose and we stop operating in our strength. The second phase is to blow up another balloon and then let the students have a great time playing with the balloon. One game is to keep the balloon in the air. Invite students to create other games as well. Dynamic activities like these also help build relationships between classmates.

Comment: Students can answer these questions in written form, with a partner, or in a brief class discussion. Encourage students to use their observation skills, the worn out balloon does not look or feel the same.

Understand: This balloon activity will show students that just as the balloon gets stretched out and weak, so do we when we follow the same routine without taking refreshing breaks. Our breaks should take us out of the daily routine, structure and environment to completely refresh us. Moving around, stretching, and interacting with others and the environment is one way to helps us renew and refresh our mind. It takes energy to

step out of the daily grinding wheel, but it is worth it.

Draw and Color: Have students make something abstract or actual of themselves playing outside with their family and friends, doing what they enjoy most in their favorite outdoor setting. Encourage them to create an image or anything that will reveal to others the importance of the place, event and/or people in their life. They can do this in the textbook or on a separate piece of paper

Reflect: Students can answer these questions individually in written format. Open a brief class discussion on the students' thoughts and answers. The purpose is to cause students to really consider how greatly their life can improve by spending time outdoors, enjoying nature in all its aspects, and seeing the beauty and opportunities that nature has to offer.
Here are 12 benefits of being outdoors:
- it improves short term memory
- it has a de-stressing effect
- it reduces inflammation in the body
- it eliminates fatigue
- it can help fight depression and anxiety
- it protects your vision (nearsightedness)
- it lowers blood pressure
- it improves your ability to focus
- it helps you be more creative
- it prevents cancer
- it boosts your immune system
- it improves your longevity
Attached is the website for more information. 4yu.info/?i=93111

Willpower

Students will understand that it is important to enjoy outdoor recreational activities on a daily basis for optimal health. They should be more motivated to enjoy themselves outside.

Lesson 13

Materials
My Best Me textbook, writing utensils, journal, paper, markers, colored pencils, crayons, origami paper for each student
* Suggestion: A great way to begin this lesson is to read the book *Oh No, George!* by Chris Haughton. You can read the story to the students, or choose 1-2 students to read aloud.

Resources
Student Worksheet: 4yu.info/?i=98313
Parent Summary: 4yu.info/?i=98363
Video: The journey of the salmon - 4yu.info/?i=93121

Glossary
incredible, current, survive, odds, amazed, unique, raging, rapids, predators, destiny, magnificent, persistence, determination, grit, circumstances, rooting, relate

Motivation
Most children know that they will be faced with difficult decisions in their lives. They have probably experienced some already at home as well as at school. When faced with hardship, we tend to choose the easy route, the one with the least resistance, or the one that feels most comfortable.

However, this is not always the best choice. For all of us, it is easy to give up on dreams, ideas, projects, and even people when things get rough, or when we experience friction, hardship, and difficulties. Choosing the right path involves resistance and obstacles to overcome, and requires courage, bravery, and determination. It is also the route that will most likely lead to tremendous satisfaction and greatness. This is hope; the courage to set goals, find pathways and build our willpower to keep going until we have achieved our set goals. Students need to learn to persevere, press in, and finish at all costs. You, as their teacher, are key to their development by setting examples, praising them for their efforts, creativity and wise choices, but above all, their persistence when the journey gets rough and obstacles have to be overcome.

13 Swimming Upstream

Goal To learn to act with courage, even when everything seems to be going against me

Pathways

Read - The Courageous Salmon

Have you ever seen video clips of salmon leaping upstream? They make an incredible trip against the current and some survive against all odds. Scientists are still amazed by their unique abilities.

Salmon are born in the fresh cold waters of fast-flowing rivers. Once they are a little older, they head out to sea and live there until they become adults. When the time comes to have babies, they return to the river where they were born. The trip back is very hard and full of many difficulties. The salmon must swim through raging rapids and waterfalls. They have to survive hitting the rocks in the rapids time and time again, free themselves from plants when they get stuck, and escape from countless predators who want to eat them, including grizzly bears! The salmon are willing to risk everything to realize their designed purpose. They must overcome many obstacles to reach their destiny and experience something magnificent. They refuse to give up!

It is important for each of us to "swim against the current" as well, especially when it is difficult. It requires strength, energy, persistence and determination (or grit) to do the right thing, even when other people and circumstances may be against us. We must act with courage to make difficult decisions and follow through with our plan.

4yu.info/?i=93121

36

Goal

To learn that courageous decisions and willpower are needed to set goals and find pathways to achieve success in life

Pathways

Read: The salmon is the reason we have the phrase, "swim upstream." Students will read this story and then be able to discuss with each other if and how they can relate to the salmon's experience. How can their life be compared to the salmon's life journey? Are they going to be brave, strong, persistent, overcome obstacles and avoid danger? Or are they going to flow down stream and give up?

Discuss the concept of listening to their "inner voice." What does that sound or look like in their life? Have they

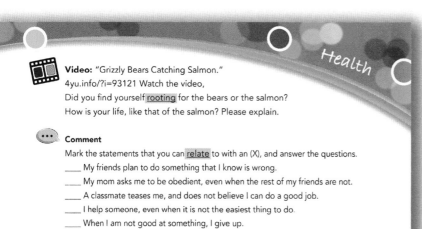

 Video: "Grizzly Bears Catching Salmon."
4yu.info/?i=93121 Watch the video,
Did you find yourself <u>rooting</u> for the bears or the salmon?
How is your life, like that of the salmon? Please explain.

Comment

Mark the statements that you can <u>relate</u> to with an (X), and answer the questions.

_____ My friends plan to do something that I know is wrong.

_____ My mom asks me to be obedient, even when the rest of my friends are not.

_____ A classmate teases me, and does not believe I can do a good job.

_____ I help someone, even when it is not the easiest thing to do.

_____ When I am not good at something, I give up.

_____ My homework is too difficult, so I don't finish.

Give an example of when you "swam against the current?"

_____

Have you followed the current (gone with the flow)? How did you feel afterward?

_____

 Activity

Make a fish with colored paper, using the origami technique. Put the fish where you can see it every day. Let it remind you to be persistent and follow your dreams. Help each other fold the fish.

Reflect

Why is it important to courageously decide to do the things that go against what everyone else is doing?

 Willpower

I am brave as I make right decisions, even if I am the only one. I have grit!

37

Allow students to come up with their own examples of situations when they needed to make brave and difficult decisions. If that stagnates, give them prompts, such as: a group of students were picking on another student; my friends were writing on the wall in the bathroom; my brother or sister turned on the TV when my parents said not to; etc. They may also consider situations where perseverance was needed: learning a new sport, studying for a test, or pushing through their fear when speaking in public.

Activity: If students have not done origami before, they may benefit from a teacher-led or student-led folding demonstration. Encourage them to hang or stand the fish in a place where they can see it daily. The fish can serve as a reminder to be brave, to be persistent, to follow their dreams, and to go against the current or flow. Have them each describe what the fish represents for them, and have them write it down, possibly on the bottom of the fish.

Reflect: Students should answer this on their own (i.e., why it's important to do things that go against the current.) It could be turned into a journal writing exercise, and expanded to include examples of a time when they themselves have been brave enough to go against the majority, or have been persistent even when faced with a difficult task. Remember, it is the small wins that will bring them to the great victories. Therefore, our attention and praise are very important for those smaller wins, as well as for helping them to recognize their development and their bigger wins.

---

experienced this voice? How? Does it tell them to do the right thing? Does it tell them not to give up? Don't forget there are different voices in the world. It might be fun to bring in two puppets (or use socks over your hands) and act out one saying, "Yes, do it!" and the other saying, "No, don't do it!" How do students know which voice to listen to? Allow the students to talk about this and figure it out amongst themselves. Assure them that the right voice will be speaking wisdom, which will give them the confidence to make the choices that lead to growth.

Video: 4yu.info/?i=93121 - Watch the video, "Grizzly Bears Catching Salmon." When do your students feel like they are swimming upstream? Why do they feel that way?

Comment: Avoid making this a judgment call. It is a good opportunity for your students to consider their own experiences and their own drive. Students will mark the descriptions they can relate to. Support them even if the decision might not be the wisest one. Stimulate a class discussion on what past decisions have taught them.

Willpower

Brave decisions birth greatness and every day heroes. Nothing is as challenging as going against the majority, and to press on to reach your goals. It creates great satisfaction and a sense of victory.

Lesson 14

Materials

My Best Me textbook, writing utensils, journal, paper, audiovisual equipment newspapers and magazines, glue, piece of colored card stock, construction paper, or computer paper
* Suggestion: A great book to read is *The Faithful Friend* by Robert D. San Souci.

Resources

Student Worksheet: 4yu.info/?i=98314
Parent Summary: 4yu.info/?i=98364
Video: A faithful friend - 4yu.info/?i=93131

Glossary

faithful, adopted, devoted, sincere, reliable, loyal, trustworthy, implies, dedication, affirmative

Motivation

Being a loyal, faithful, true friend requires a consistent display of dedication, sincerity and love toward another person even when, at times, they are unpleasant and might not see or appreciate all that you are doing for them.

If you are a true friend, you keep your promises (your word), practice active listening skills, accept others with their flaws and strengths, are quick to forgive and ask forgiveness, honestly speak your opinion at an appropriate time without letting it affect your relationship, and are there for them in good times and bad. Commitment and friendship are being watered down more and more. Therefore, it is important for students to identify and put into practice the traits and characteristics of strong friendships. The more they practice being a faithful friend, the more likely they will be able to overcome challenges and experience the joys that a faithful friendship can bring.

Students will understand that having trustworthy friends who they can reach out to and being a trustworthy friend not only makes life more fun, makes them more healthy, but also brings with it confidence and fulfillment. Have students reflect on their personal friendship qualities.

14 Faithful Friend

Goal To learn that a friend is **faithful**

Pathways

 Read

After you read the story, put each part in the correct order from 1 to 3

____ The teacher never appeared, but Hachiko waited 10 years for him until he was no longer able to travel to the station. Today, there is a statue of Hachiko at the train station as an example of faithfulness.

____ There once was a teacher in Japan who **adopted** a puppy and called him Hachiko. Every day, the dog would accompany the teacher to the train station and wait there for his return. After a year, the affection between the teacher and Hachiko had grown very strong. They were the best of friends.

____ One afternoon, the teacher did not get off the train. He had passed away. However, day after day, not minding the weather, Hachiko appeared at the station waiting for the teacher.

Now read the story from the beginning to the end.

 Comment

Why is it said that a dog is man's best friend?
What problems did Hachiko have to face?
How did he show he was a faithful friend?
What do you think of when you hear the word faithful?

 Understand

Hachiko was a faithful dog because he was **devoted** and true to his friend. He

40

Goal

To discover what true friendship is and if the trait of faithfulness applies to each student and to their friends and classmates

Pathways

Read: Students will individually and silently read each part of the 3-part story about Hachiko, the faithful dog, and number the story parts in order from 1-3. The story exemplifies faithfulness, and gives students a clear example of what it means to be a true friend. Review this activity and their answers with them.

Comment: Students may answer these questions in written form or discuss them with a partner, in a small group, or as a class. You can also invite students to share their own experiences of being a faithful friend

Community

loved his owner and he did not let circumstances of the weather or time influence his actions. Someone who is faithful is sincere and reliable, loyal and trustworthy. Faithfulness implies dedication and devotion. It means standing up for another person, a cause, an idea or a belief, even when it is difficult to do so.

Create

You will draw the name of one classmate out of a hat. Shhhhh!!!! Don't say the name out loud! Write letters in all capitals and then cut and paste them on a self-made card or piece of paper in order to create a secret, positive message for that student. Even if this person is not a close friend, encourage each other and stand by one another as classmates. Find affirmative things to say about your classmate and let them know through this secret message! Give the message to your teacher and he or she will pass it out to the correct person.

Reflect

Was it hard for you to create this message? Why or why not?
How did you feel when you read the message written to you?
Please give an example of you being faithful to a friend or family member.
How can you commit to being more faithful? Write down three ideas.

1. ____________________
2. ____________________
3. ____________________

Video: 4yu.info/?i=93131
Here is another story about a faithful dog. Watch this clip and be inspired to be a faithful friend.

4yu.info/?i=93131

Willpower

I am always faithful to my friends and family.

41

and having trustworthy friends in their lives. What made these friends so special, and what makes you so special as a loyal friend? Have you had any friends who betrayed you? Have you ever betrayed a friend? How could this have been avoided? How did you feel when your friends were unfaithful to you? How did you feel when you were unfaithful to your friends? Did they apologize? Did you apologize? Try to keep a discussion going as they explore what the trait of faithfulness is all about.

Understand: Have a student read this section to the class. Take time with your students to continue to discover and define what true friendship implies and why it is so valuable. Have students explain each trait that is mentioned and give an example.

Create: Privately assign students a classmate by allowing them to pull a name out of a hat. Have students write a secret note to their chosen classmate using newspapers and magazines (if you have them available). They can tear out letters from newspapers and/or magazines to "write" their message by tearing or cutting the letters out of the pages. If you don't have magazines and newspapers available, have students develop their own letters on colored paper and cut them out to paste on their message. Encourage them to take their time in planning the message in order to create something special for the other person, even if they are not a close friend. Explain that the idea is to write a positive, encouraging, supportive message to the other student. They can point out the student's strengths, what they like about him or her, and why they enjoy being in class with that student. They can also give words of encouragement about an activity he or she is involved in, etc. The recipient should feel supported and uplifted when he or she reads the message. It might be wise to collect them first, read them and then hand them out the next time.

Reflect: Students will have the opportunity to reflect on the creation of the letter or note to their classmate. Students should answer on their own first, then share with a partner or small group. End the time by having students focus on how they can improve their level of faithfulness toward others by writing down 3 points that they can work on.

Ask students to reflect on the impact their created card had on their classmate. Let students share what they experienced receiving a card from their classmates.

Video: 4yu.info/?i=93131
This video clip is about Shep the dog, similar to the Hachiko story. Have the students watch it as a closing of the lesson.

Willpower

It is valuable for a student's personal wellbeing to always make the choice of being a faithful, loyal and true friend, even when others don't behave in this manner.

Lesson 15

Materials

My Best Me textbook, writing utensils, journal, paper, audiovisual equipment highlighter for each student, red, yellow, and green poster paper to display the class results, 3 pieces of card stock or smaller pieces of colored paper, or sticky notes for each group
* Suggestion: Read *Do Unto Otters: A Book About Manners* by Laurie Keller.

Resources

Student Worksheet: 4yu.info/?i=98315
Parent Summary: 4yu.info/?i=98365

Glossary

gentle, insult, attentively, considerate, gentle, judge, criticize, distracted, disrupt

Motivation

When children come to school, they are merged with a diverse group of other people. Within this mixture of diverse people will be students who have been explicitly and implicitly taught different behaviors, some of which might be strange, offensive and even dangerous to others. Students who may have grown up in adverse circumstances, might demonstrate disruptive behaviors because they don't know how to behave correctly in class (skills they never learned.) The great diversity of this random assortment of students increases the challenge of establishing a safe and welcoming classroom environment where children feel free to be themselves, while respecting each other's individual needs. A classroom culture where respect and trust are highly valued will enhance the learning process in your classroom. Who better to help you do this than the students themselves. The classroom expectations, rules and norms, get a life of their own when students are involved in the creation of the classroom culture, because this puts a gentle demand on students to take ownership for their actions.

Goal To learn to respect the learning environment in my classroom

Pathways

Comment
Read the words in the table below and circle the words that describe you. Explain why.

nice	respectful	gentle
helpful	considerate	polite
kind	warm and friendly	thoughtful
open	interested in others' ideas	accepting of others

Read - My Classmates

My classmates are cool, there is no one I want to insult,
I prefer to treat them **nicely**, **attentively**, and **politely**.
I like my classmates, I don't want to bother them,
I prefer to be **helpful**, **considerate** and **gentle**.
My classmates are cool, there is no one I want to anger or hurt,
I prefer to be **kind**, **friendly**, and **thoughtful**.
I like my classmates, I don't want to judge and criticize,
I want to be **open**, **interested**, and **accepting**.

Write
Create your own sentences with at least six of the highlighted words and share them with the class. If you don't know the meaning, look it up.

_____

_____

42

Goal

To learn to identify and display respectful classroom behavior and contribute to a constructive learning environment

Pathways

Comment: Students will look at the words in the table, consider which ones describe them, and then, circle those words. You could also ask them to circle the words that describe the classroom environment with a different color.

Read: Read the passage aloud and verify that students clearly understand the words and sentences written. How does the passage inspire them to increase their level of respect toward their classmates as well as their teacher?

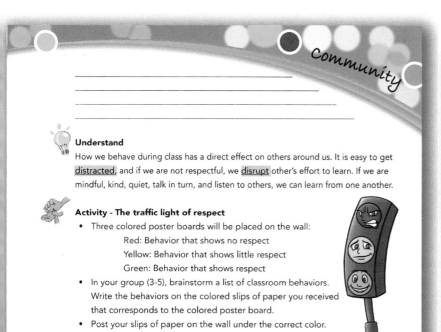

_____

_____

_____

_____

 Understand

How we behave during class has a direct effect on others around us. It is easy to get distracted, and if we are not respectful, we disrupt other's effort to learn. If we are mindful, kind, quiet, talk in turn, and listen to others, we can learn from one another.

 Activity - The traffic light of respect

- Three colored poster boards will be placed on the wall:

    Red: Behavior that shows no respect

    Yellow: Behavior that shows little respect

    Green: Behavior that shows respect

- In your group (3-5), brainstorm a list of classroom behaviors. Write the behaviors on the colored slips of paper you received that corresponds to the colored poster board.

- Post your slips of paper on the wall under the correct color.

 Draw

Write your promised behavior on a piece of paper. In the classroom I promise to:

_____

Name: _____   Signature: _____

Reflect

Have I had moments in which I lacked respect for my teacher and classmates? How can I be more helpful and useful in my learning environment?

Willpower

I want everyone in my class to be able to learn. I will respect my classroom learning environment.

43

The highlighted words all contribute to building respect; the basic aspect required for building a healthy and safe learning environment in which students can thrive and flourish. Respect, however, takes on a life of its own depending on who is defining it, as it is greatly influenced by a student's family, culture, and belief system. Therefore, make sure all your students agree on one definition for the word respect while they operate and function inside the classroom.

Remember that you, as the teacher, are the best example of what respect looks like, especially toward students who don't show you respect.

Write: Students have the opportunity to use 6 of the words in bold in the passage to create their own sentences based on their own life experience. This is a chance for them to think about how these words fit into their classroom experience. Remind them that this can be an opportunity to put their goals and expectations of their classmates, and even of you as their teacher, into words. If they are struggling, give them some prompts:

How should you treat your classmates? Who deserves respect? Why do you respect your classmates? Let them work with a partner if they need to bounce ideas off of each other.

Understand: Give an opportunity for students to share their sentences if they want to. Make sure everyone understands how disrespect and impoliteness affects the entire class.

Activity: Post 3 pieces of colored poster paper on the wall: red, yellow, and green. In small groups, students will brainstorm various classroom behaviors that they feel would fit into the 3 categories of respect. Remind them that there may be varying opinions among group members and that the differences offer an opportunity to promote healthy discussion. When finished, students will post their lists on the board under the correct color. Discuss as a class the similarities and differences among the lists. As a class, select 10 priorities that will give guidelines for respect in the classroom.

Draw: Now students will commit to a practical action that demonstrates respect; a promise to the class giving classmates permission to hold them accountable to the promise made.

Reflect: Students should be able to tie consequences to their respectful or disrespectful behavior. By focusing on themselves, students should become more aware of living up to the class' expectations. It would be valuable to have students openly participate in this process of outlining the consequences. Judging others is easy; judging yourself can be challenging.

Willpower

Students should understand the importance of showing themselves and others respect at all times, and in so doing, increase the learning potential for themselves and others.

Lesson 16

Materials

My Best Me textbook, writing utensils, journal, paper, audiovisual equipment small pieces of paper with animal names (enough for each student), another set of small pieces of paper with students' names written on each one, a hat or deep bowl to put the names in and draw from.

* Suggestion: A great way to begin this lesson is to read the book *Hey Little Ant* by Phillip M. Hoose, Hannah Hoose, and Debbie Tilley.

Resources

Student Worksheet: 4yu.info/?i=98316
Parent Summary: 4yu.info/?i=98366
Video: Empathy - 4yu.info/?i=93151

Glossary

descriptions, represent, styles, distinct, cultures, personalities, empathy, compassion

Motivation

The skill of developing healthy relationships with people around us, is tied to the skills of exhibiting sincere interest in others, showing them love, and acting upon our intuition to help them. A wonderful way for students to develop and practice their skills of caring for others is to imaginatively put themselves in another person's shoes and practice awareness of that person's life and background. Get to know their likes and dislikes to better understand them, and be prepared to assist them when they need someone or something.

Developing skills, like empathy, compassion, consideration, etc. will help students avoid offending or bothering each other, because they have developed greater understanding. Instead of judging and criticizing each other, putting effort into discovering who the other person is, will be far more valuable and productive. Once they learn to be mindful on a consistent basis, they will become change agents who make the people around them flourish and be confident. This elevates the classroom culture as joy and satisfaction increase. Students will discover the powerful, positive impact they have on others.

16 In Your Shoes

Goal To learn to put myself in someone else's shoes

Pathways

Game

What am I?
- Choose a piece of paper out of the hat and silently read the name of the animal written on the paper.
- Without sound, act out the animal you picked in front of the class.
- The class will guess which animal you are acting out.

Who am I?
- Choose a piece of paper out of the hat and silently read the student's name written on the paper.
- Write down three positive descriptions about your classmate and two things your classmate likes and give to the teacher.
- The teacher will read your description to the class, (keeping their name secret).
  "I am _____, _____, and _____."
  "I like _____ and _____."
- The class will guess who you described.

Comment

While acting, did you feel like the animal? Did you represent your classmate well?
Did your classmates guess which animal you were?
Did your classmates guess which student you described?
Which of the two presentations was easier for you to do?

Understand

Life is fun and interesting because we are all different. We have different interests, a

Goal

The students will develop mindfulness to be able to better understand and appreciate others and how they operate with their likes and dislikes

Pathways

Game: Students will role-play 2 different games. In the first round, students will choose an animal at random and act it out in front of the class. This helps break the ice. Other students will have the opportunity to guess which animal is being presented.

The second round will include pulling a student's name out of a bag. Each student will write 3 words that describe that classmate (on the slip of paper) and 2 things that classmate likes. This will give the students an opportunity to put effort into thinking and discovering the likes and characteristics of their

variety of _styles_, _distinct_ _cultures_ and beliefs, and unique _personalities_. _Empathy_ and _compassion_ are skills that we need when we relate to others. Empathy is when we understand the difficulties others face every day, what they like or what bothers them, and why they act and react the way they do in each situation. Compassion is when we show them sincere love and are gentle in how we react.

Video: 4yu.info/?i=93151

What can empathy bring to you?

Why did the young man help those people?

What did he get out of it? What did they receive?

4yu.info/?i=93151

Activity - Buddy Challenge

1. Mark from the list the three things that bother you the most:

☐ Someone takes my supplies out without my permission.
☐ Someone breaks my supplies.
☐ Someone calls me nicknames.
☐ Being pushed in line.
☐ Being blamed for something I didn't do.

☐ Someone doesn't do what I ask.
☐ Being hit.
☐ Being screamed at.
☐ Being lied to.
☐ Not being answered.
☐ Not being listened to.
☐ Other: _____

2. Read your dislikes to a classmate.

3. Lookup the words "empathy" and "compassion" in the dictionary.

4. For the rest of the day, watch out for your buddy. Show empathy and compassion when things they don't like happen to them. Make sure you help your buddy.

Reflect

Does everyone like and dislike the same things?

Were you able to help your partner today? How?

Can you understand your classmate better after recognizing his or her dislikes?

Willpower

My empathy for my classmates deepens and develops as I better understand them.

45

---

classmate. You might want to brainstorm positive descriptions ahead of time, and have a list visible during the activity. Remind students to use positive descriptions of their classmates. Encourage them to think of compliments and descriptions they like to hear about themselves when writing for their classmate.

Comment: Students can reflect upon the role-playing activity in a small or large group setting. Discover if students found it difficult to describe their classmate and why they might have found it difficult.

Understand: Before reading this section, allow time to discuss the meaning of the words "empathy" and "compassion." Find the definitions in the glossary or the attached link. Sometimes, the best way to discover the value of what it feels like when someone is thoughtful toward you is to think of moments when we wished we would have had somebody understand us better.

Video: 4yu.info/?i=93151

Keep in mind that this video is in Thai, with English subtitles. Though the plot is straightforward, and does not need many words to explain it, if students are confused, have another student describe what is happening. Then have them respond to the questions in their workbooks or as a class.

Activity: Have each student mark 3 of the situations mentioned in the chart which bother them the most. Students can write down other examples if they wish. Then have them select a partner and share with one another their dislikes. Give them time to explain to each other why these things bother them so much, so that the other student can better understand what is going on. What do they feel and experience on the inside when these things happen to them.

The next step is a buddy challenge in which the paired-up students will look out for each others' interests and wellbeing. This activity can be done for a small period of time or for an entire school day. Remind the students that the purpose of the activity is to feel what it is like to practice caring and being responsible for someone else. Help students understand that help and care can go beyond the marked and observed items in the chart. Inspire the paired up students to really do their best looking out for each other.

Reflect: Feel free to have students answer in written form or hold a class discussion. This is a great time for students to entrust their thoughts to their journal. Give them time to think and put into words the feelings and thoughts they have concerning this topic and activity.

Willpower

The more students understand each other, the more care and consideration they will have for one another. Invite students to share their thoughts about the Willpower statement in their textbooks, and discuss how they will put the concept into practice.

Lesson 17

Materials

My Best Me textbook, writing utensils, journal, paper, audiovisual equipment
*Suggestion: A great way to begin this lesson is to read the book *Strictly No Elephants* by Lisa Mantchev and Tae-eun Yoo. You can read the book to the class.

Resources

Student Worksheet: 4yu.info/?i=98317
Parent Summary: 4yu.info/?i=98367
Video: Acts of Kindness - 4yu.info/?i=93161

Glossary

capable, maze, lend, donate, accompany, uncomfortable, ashamed, sensitivity

Motivation

Students will learn that helping others is not only a key aspect of being a constructive member of society, but it also increases our personal joy, satisfaction and confidence. Helping each other makes the world all around a healthier and better place. Helping actions positively impact the person being helped, the helper, as well as the entire community because they cause a ripple effect of goodwill. It is not always easy to offer our help, especially when we do not know the person or do not know what to do. We can feel intimidated, embarrassed, and uncomfortable reaching out to others. Nevertheless, lending a helping hand shows that we care for others and that makes the world a more joyful place, which includes your classroom.

Students will need to develop their skills in observation and be attentive to their environment. They should be able to identify people who need help. It can be hard to receive help and it can be difficult to ask for help or extend it. Many people don't ask for help because they don't want to inconvenience others, make them feel uncomfortable or embarrassed, or many other reasons. Students should learn to tactfully extend their help when they are confronted with others' needs. School is a good place to learn and develop this praiseworthy habit.

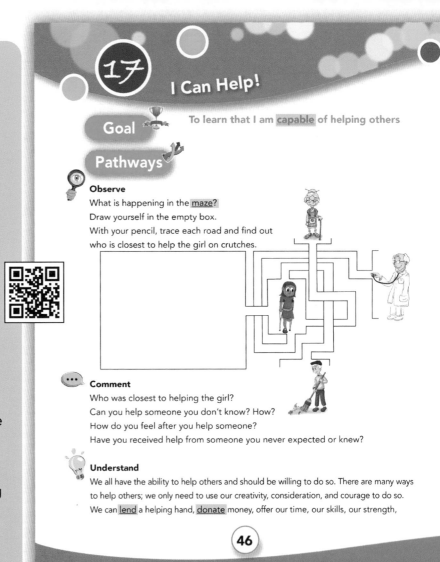

17 I Can Help!

Goal To learn that I am capable of helping others

Pathways

Observe
What is happening in the maze?
Draw yourself in the empty box.
With your pencil, trace each road and find out who is closest to help the girl on crutches.

Comment
Who was closest to helping the girl?
Can you help someone you don't know? How?
How do you feel after you help someone?
Have you received help from someone you never expected or knew?

Understand
We all have the ability to help others and should be willing to do so. There are many ways to help others; we only need to use our creativity, consideration, and courage to do so. We can lend a helping hand, donate money, offer our time, our skills, our strength,

46

Goal

To understand that the ability and willingness to help others is a major thought paradigm shift which will bring them in contact with people with needs

Pathways

 **Observe:** Students will work out the maze. Who needs help? What kind of help might they need. Have students draw themselves in the empty box. Students will complete the maze to see who is closest to the girl on crutches. This brings us to an ethical question. If we are the closest, are able and see a need, but we don't help; what have we become?

Comment: This is an invitation for students to share their personal experiences and feelings about helping others. It might be best to start off asking if they

give a word of encouragement, <u>accompany</u> others in difficult moments, or visit the sick. Sometimes the person who needs and receives our help can feel <u>uncomfortable</u> or <u>ashamed</u>. Have you ever felt too scared or ashamed to ask for help? It is important that when we offer our help, we do it with <u>sensitivity</u> toward the other person's feelings.

Video - Watch: Color Your World With Kindness
How did the characters help each other and show kindness?
What is one small act of kindness you can do today?
4yu.info/?i=93161

4yu.info/?i=93161

Observe
Underneath each image, and in one word, write a creative idea of how to help

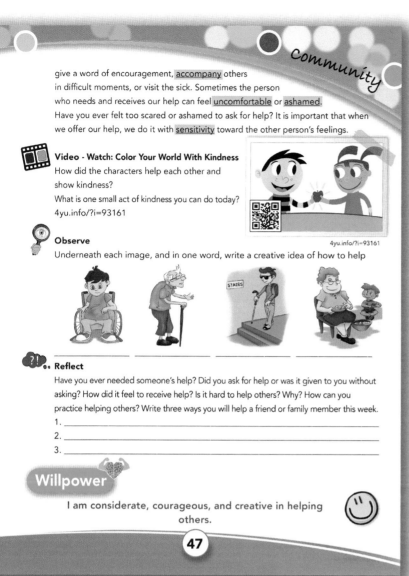

_____ _____ _____ _____

Reflect
Have you ever needed someone's help? Did you ask for help or was it given to you without asking? How did it feel to receive help? Is it hard to help others? Why? How can you practice helping others? Write three ways you will help a friend or family member this week.
1. _____
2. _____
3. _____

Willpower

I am considerate, courageous, and creative in helping others.

47

---

ever received help and what their experience was with that. Ask them if they have ever helped others. If not, why not; or if they have, why did they help and how did it go. Discuss how to help strangers in a safe manner. End with students sharing their experiences and feelings of asking for help when they needed it. Did they ask a stranger or someone they knew.

Remind them of the word empathy, and to consider helping other students who they may not normally interact with. Encourage them to be a help in the classroom as well as in the school. Take time to think about how helping one another influences our community, our society and ourselves.

Understand: Before reading, brainstorm ways to help others. This can be done either as a whole class or in small groups. Start with the classroom and school environment and how they can be of greater help to their classmates, other students and school staff. It is important to make the experience of helping others an easy and pleasant habit to develop; one that is celebrated. Write

the ideas down on the white board and make a picture of it when it's done, as a reminder. You might consider turning the list into posters (photos) that are visible in the classroom or in the hallway.

Video: 4yu.info/?i=93161 - Watch the video as a class: "Color Your World with Kindness" Encourage your students to discuss specific steps they can take to better "color their world with kindness."

Observe and Write: Have students intently look at the images. What needs do they think these individuals might have? It could be more than one. Underneath each image in the textbook, have students write a creative idea of how to help. Students will create their own captions on how they can help the people in each picture. If students finish early, have them create their own examples.

Reflect: Students can reflect in written form or discuss in a small or large group. Remind students to actively be on the look-out for opportunities in and out of the classroom to help others. Discuss obstacles that might prevent them from helping others. How can they overcome them? Be sure they write their answers to the last question and commit to helping in 3 different ways. Encourage them to be realistic in their plans. Check back on their progress the following week to see how the habit of helping others is developing in their lives. Invite students to share their experiences to stir up the atmosphere and increase the desire in others to help. Follow-up is key, as well as celebrating their small victories.

Willpower

It is important to know how to help others in a tactful manner. Students should understand that it will require them to be brave, wise and creative. Helping others, is helping yourself.

Lesson 18

Materials

My Best Me textbook, writing utensils, journal, paper, audiovisual equipment, written examples of conflict for each group of 5 students, tangled ropes or strings for groups of 2 to 3 students
* Suggestion: A great way to begin this lesson is to read the book *The Day the Crayons Quit* by Drew Daywalt and Oliver Jeffers.

Resources

Student Worksheet: 4yu.info/?i=98318
Parent Summary: 4yu.info/?i=98368

Glossary

strategy, untangle, yanks, anxious, conflicts, moderator, referee, irritated

Motivation

Conflict is inevitable in any relationship, and it can be uncomfortable and even detrimental if it is not dealt with or handled properly. At an early age, students should start developing the skill of conflict resolution so they are able to responsibly and confidently manage problems and challenges as they arise, and doing it promptly (i.e.,"don't let the sun go down on your anger.")

Many of the students can be uncomfortable applying this skill because confrontation is generally uncomfortable for most people. However, this does not imply it has to get out of control. Another aspect that is so often intertwined with conflict is the fear of rejection, which can cause individuals to deny, avoid, postpone or cover up the conflicts they have in their life.

However, the longer the friction exists, the greater the agitation becomes. Resolving conflicts requires that someone is humble enough to take the first step, whether guilty or not.

It can be effective to provide your students with real-life examples and strategies of conflict resolution. One approach is to role-play ways to be an active listener, to be vulnerable, to use "I ... statements, etc. while managing our feelings in a calm and respectful way.

18 Let's Talk About It

Goal

To learn to solve conflicts calmly

Pathways

 Activity
In small groups, untangle the rope you were given.

 Comment
Who was able to untangle it first?
Did you use a strategy to untangle the rope? Please explain.
Did you like untangling the rope?
Did your classmates in your group like untangling the rope?
Who was the best at untangling the rope in your group? Why?
Was it better to untangle it calmly or to try to hurry and finish first?

 Read
Julio has several pencils in his desk. Emily doesn't have a pencil to do her homework, so she goes over to Julio's desk and takes one without asking. She returns to her desk while Julio runs over to her desk and yanks it out of her hands.

 Comment
In this story, was there anyone at fault? Please explain.
How would you solve the problem(s) presented in this story?
How could the problem(s) presented have been avoided?
If you had this experience, what would you have done? Why?

💡 **Understand**
If we were anxious, irritated or in a hurry when we untangled the rope, we probably

48

Goal

The students will improve their skills of conflict resolution by becoming calm and active listeners, bold enough to address unsettled issues in their life

Pathways

Activity: Students will untangle knotted rope or strings. They may do this in groups of 2 to 3 students. Try to have the ropes equally tangled, so that each group has the same task. You can ask 1 to 2 students to tangle the ropes a day before this lesson. Let students know it is not a race.

During the activity, observe the students' behaviors and the way they untangle their rope, as well as their reaction to others during the activity. Are they taking their time and remaining calm, or are they easily frustrated? Are

tangled it more. If the girl in the drawing combs her hair quickly and impatiently, it will really hurt her and she will make little or no progress.

Conflicts with classmates and friends are like knots and tangles, and they should be approached and solved in the same way; little by little and with patience. It is a healthy habit to talk about our conflicts. When we take the time to solve a conflict, we should give each person involved the opportunity to share his/her thoughts. Then, we should recognize what the other person said, decide on the best solution, and apply it. At times, we may need a referee to help us come to an agreement.

Activity

- Form a group of five.
- Make 2 teams of 2 and the 5th person will be a moderator (referee).
- You will be given an example of a classroom conflict by your teacher.
- Practice discussing and resolving the conflict in a calm way.
- Present your experience to the class.

Reflect

Is it easier to resolve conflicts with a referee? Why?
Is it easier to be calm or show anger?
Am I able to solve problems when I am anxious?
How do I remain calm when I feel irritated? List three ways.

1. ______________________________
2. ______________________________
3. ______________________________

Willpower

I will resolve conflicts by listening to others and using calm words.

49

they working together, or is one student taking over?

You might choose to end the activity even if they have not all untangled their ropes. Use your own discretion, and don't let frustrations escalate too much.

Comment: Students will have the opportunity to respond in writing or in a discussion. Encourage them to reflect on the activity, the effort and the way in which they conquered the task. If they had to do it again, would they do it the same way? If they changed something, what would it be? What was the number one thing they learned as they were untangling the rope or strings. What advice would they give someone who had to untangle a rope?

Read: This is a short story regarding a conflict in the classroom. Verify with your students if this story is relatable. If the story is not relatable ask them to share their experience of a conflict at school or maybe even in the classroom as a practical and prompt example of bringing that conflict to a solution.

Comment: Students will have the opportunity to discuss the story. Feel free to talk about it as a class. Many students may have their own personal experiences to share of similar situations and how they dealt with the situation. Let the discussion flow and make sure everyone has an opportunity to express themselves. Keep students directed to bringing the friction, challenge or problem to a solution, not fanning the flames.

Understand: Be mindful of any students who may be struggling to understand the concept of conflict resolution. For some, this may be a totally new idea and even threating. Explain that resolving a conflict is not about "winning," but about understanding the other person's position, even if we don't agree with them.

Activity: Students will be role-playing examples of common classroom conflicts in order to properly practice conflict resolution. It is important that each student have the opportunity to be on both sides of the conflict resolution. Conflicts may include, but are not limited to:

- A student knocks over another student's drink
- One student is being left out of a group
- A student accidentally trips another student
- Two students want to use the same book (or other school supply)
- Pairs can't agree on a topic for their project
- A student uses rough and destructive words with another student

Reflect: Let students think about what happens inside of them when there are conflicts, when trying to solve a conflict, when a conflict has been resolved, and when it has not.

Willpower

Some of the best keys to apply with conflict resolution is to stay calm, listen attentively and talk toward a solution; discuss how to put the conflict behind you.

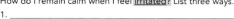

Lesson 19

Materials

My Best Me textbook, writing utensils, journal, paper, audiovisual equipment
* Suggestion: A great way to begin this lesson is to read the book *Being Trustworthy: A Book About Trustworthiness* by Mary Small.

Resources

Student Worksheet: 4yu.info/?i=98319
Parent Summary: 4yu.info/?i=98369
Video: The Lion and the Mouse - 4yu.info/?i=93181

Glossary

phrase, corresponding, promise, gain, dependable, humored, gnawing, endured, trial,

Motivation

Trustworthiness is a valuable character trait that helps us form and maintain strong relationships with family and friends. It will give us favor with strangers and influential people. Trust is something that takes time to build but can be broken in an instant. Students need to understand that trust is built when their actions line up with their words at all times. It also means that when their actions and words fail to line up, for one reason or another, they immediately take responsibility, humbly recognize the discrepancy, apologize for not being true to their word, and make amends. An emphasis on trustworthiness and following through on their word encourages students to be true, honest, and loyal; not only with others, but also with themselves.

There is a saying that goes, "You are only as good as your word." Words project our intentions and convictions, because they carry and transmit a message, and are a reflection of who we are. We want to encourage students to think before speaking, and to consider how their words might impact those around them. When the messages we speak are backed up with equitable actions, they become a powerful force bringing into existence the things they stand for. Words are potent!

19   I Do What I Say

Goal   To understand that others trust me when I do what I say I will do

Pathways

Draw
Put the phrase in the correct order. Write the words in the corresponding boxes.

♥ Do cannot keep that make promises not you

Do not make promises that you cannot keep

Define "promise" _____

 Comment
What does the phrase on the train mean?
What is expected when you give your word? Why?
Have you ever made a promise and not kept it?
Has someone ever promised you something and didn't follow through? How did you feel?

Understand
What do you think of when you hear the word trust? To grow, mature, and have an impact on others, we need people to trust us. Trust is something we gain over time, when our words and actions match. Someone is dependable when they do what they say. That is why we keep our promises no matter how unimportant they may seem. This shows, in a powerful way, that we value ourselves and others because we consider our words to be important.

50

 **Goal**

To understand that trust is a treasure and realize that an honest and trustworthy person does what they say and say what they mean at all times

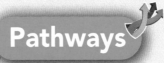 **Pathways**

Draw: Students will complete the phrase. Have students define the word "promise" (definition in glossary) and share it with a partner. The definitions will likely vary from each other, which will make it interesting.

 Comment: Students may answer these questions in written form or in a discussion. As you discuss the subject of keeping a promise or your word, make sure all the students understand the concept. This subject might disclose a situation in which students have been asked to do something that is unhealthy, dangerous or even illegal,

Community

Video:
Watch the clip first and then read the story.
4yu.info/?i=93181

4yu.info/?i=93181

 Read

One day, a hungry lion caught a mouse to eat. The mouse begged: "Please, oh king of the animals, let me go! I am too small to still your hunger. If you let me go, one day I will be able to help you." The lion roared with laughter: "Help me, you weak, small creature? You humored me so I will not eat you." With that said, the lion let the mouse go. Time passed until one day the lion was caught in a thick net. He roared in anger but could not escape. The mouse heard his roar and knew the jungle king was in trouble. He ran as fast as he could to find the lion. Then with his teeth, the mouse started gnawing at the rope. He chewed, bit and tugged until it broke. At last, the lion was able to escape through the gap to freedom. That day, the mouse and the lion became good friends, with a trust that endured any trial.

 Comment

Did the mouse keep his word?
How does this story help you understand the importance of trust?

 Activity

Do you trust your classmates? How can you become more trustworthy? Meet in groups of 3-4 to talk about what trust means to you.

Reflect

Are you able to put your trust in your classmates? Why or why not?
How do I gain people's trust?

 Willpower

I will be trustworthy, always keeping my word.

51

being sworn to secrecy or cooperation. Help students discover how to correctly deal with these situations, because it does not mean they have to stay silent. Trust does not mean covering up inappropriate and dangerous behavior or threats. Trust and confidentiality training at this age must be simple. Secrets about hurtful things should be shared with adults. Happy surprises can be kept secret.

Understand: Read this section aloud. As you read it stop at times to evaluate if what is being read is understood by the students. Have students think about themselves. Do their words and actions line up?

Video: 4yu.info/?i=93181 - Watch the video to prepare to talk about the Aesop's Fable, "The Lion and the Mouse."

Read: Students will read the short Aesop's Fable about the lion and the mouse, and how the mouse kept his promise. By keeping his promise, the mouse was faithful to the lion and faithful to himself.

Comment: Discuss the story. Have your students make connections to their own lives. Have people broken their promises to them? How did that feel?

Activity: Option 1: Trust Fall - Have students divide into groups of 3. Two students stand behind another student, all three facing forward, so that the students in the back are looking at the back of the student in front of them. The student in the front will fall backwards, trusting that the other students will catch him/her. Divide the students in such a manner that they will be able to catch each other and hold each other. Show them how to fall back slowly and carefully, not suddenly. Give instructions to your class to avoid accidents. Have students commit to catching each other. Option 2: Trust Walk - Students will do this activity in pairs. One student will wear a blindfold while the other student will lead them around the room, or ideally, around a simple obstacle course set up in the gym or on the playground. Make sure students look out for each other and don't do anything silly or dangerous. Remind them that the intent of the game is to gain the trust of their fellow student.

Reflect: How did the students feel when they put their trust in their classmates? This could bring issues to the surface that exist in how students relate one to another. Issues related to trust will need to be addressed carefully. This topic may be sensitive to the students, so give them the option to respond in journal form.

 Willpower

Verify if students believe that being trustworthy is important and how that will take shape in their life. What will that look like?

49

Lesson 20

Materials

My Best Me textbook, writing utensils, journal, paper, audiovisual equipment, markers, crayons, colored pencils, glue, magazines, scissors, large poster paper, access to library or Internet

* Suggestion: A great way to begin this lesson is to read the book *Wonderful Nature, Wonderful You* by Karin Ireland.

* Suggestion: Here is an interesting video that focus on food chains and life cycles that could help give students better insight into these subjects. - 4yu.info/?i=93202

Resources

Student Worksheet: 4yu.info/?i=98320
Parent Summary: 4yu.info/?i=98370
Video: Food Chains - 4yu.info/?i=93201

Glossary

caterpillars, development, complex, extensive, endanger, extent, habitats, adequate

Motivation

Every living creature is part of a life or food cycle. These cycles keep the world healthy, balanced and operating. Calling them life cycles is very revealing; each creature gets to live and then through their death/life provide nutrients for other creatures. Sometimes this may seem harsh, but these cycles are the essence of living.

Students might not understand that every living creature helps maintain the fine balance in nature and that each life cycle has a unique purpose and function in our natural environment. All creatures exist because they contribute to the overall picture.

The only creatures responsible for taking care of the environment, maintaining its balance and not interrupting the existing cycles are humans. We are the only creature that greatly profits from all the resources in our environment in more ways than only nurturing ourselves. Most creatures live to eat and reproduce. Humans live for far more than just eating and reproducing.

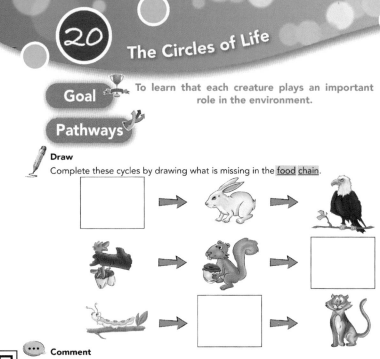

20 The Circles of Life

Goal To learn that each creature plays an important role in the environment.

Pathways

Draw

Complete these cycles by drawing what is missing in the food chain.

Comment

What would happen if there weren't any creatures that ate rabbits?
What would happen if caterpillars or acorns were not eaten by other creatures?
Where do you belong in the food chain?

Understand

Life is often presented as a circle because it seems to wrap around like a loop. When one creature dies it becomes a nutrition source for other living creatures, and therefore, produces life. In nature, each plant and every creature functions and has its place in the food and life cycles that exist. The grass has a life cycle of

54

Goal

To identify various life and food cycles as parts of the whole picture and to be able to define their purpose and understand the unique management role humans have

Pathways

 **Draw:** Students will fill in the gaps in the food chains (food cycles) displayed. Answers can vary. If they are having trouble, allow them to work in groups or pairs.

Comment: Students may know much or little about the details and importance of the food chain and life cycles, and their relationship to the environment. Allow students to teach each other by building off of each other's background knowledge to answer the questions.

its own and, at the same time, is part of a greater cycle, in which it feeds the rabbits. The rabbits have their own cycle of development, yet they feed the eagle and, therefore, are part of a more complex life cycle. Each living creature is necessary and forms part of this beautiful world, which is sustained by these different life cycles.

We are also part of these life cycles, and because of our abilities, we use nature and its living creatures in far more extensive ways than just for food. We greatly profit from all the resources that are available in our environment to an extent that, if we are not careful, we can endanger those cycles. Therefore, people are the only creatures that have the full responsibility of caring for the natural environment in a wise and balanced way so that it will not be destroyed. We have the ability to carefully protect living creatures, their habitats, and their life cycles so that all of nature continues to operate and function. In this world where "the big eat the small," we, as the "biggest," should operate and manage these riches with great care.

 Apply
Food Chains: Go on the Internet and do some research about food chains. With a partner, create a poster representing what you discovered. You may draw pictures, print them from the Internet, or cut them out of magazines.

 Reflect
What is my role inside the circles of life? Why am I valuable? Have we done an adequate job of taking care of the natural environment? Why or why not?

 Willpower

I take care of my natural environment to maintain the balance of all the life cycles around me.

💡 **Understand:** Have students take turns in reading this section. Students will enhance their understanding of how each creature in the food chain holds a significant role in the organizational structure of nature. The concept that human beings have a greater responsibility than other creatures to take care of the environment may be a new concept for some. Nevertheless, help students understand they are also the biggest consumers of all that nature provides. Prompt students to ask questions, if need be, especially on this idea of human stewardship of the planet. When students become more aware of what is happening in their environment, they will become more involved. Information empowers and motivates us to participate in bringing change

👍 **Apply:** Students should have access to the library or the Internet to research food chains. 4yu.info/?i=93201 With a partner, the students will create a poster depicting a food chain. They can draw their own pictures, cut pictures out of magazines, or print

images from the Internet. If possible, it would also be fun for them to take photos of plants or animals in their environment and print them out to use on their posters. This will hopefully make them more aware of all the life cycles that surround them.

Allow there to be interactions between the different groups of students. When they, in their excitement, share and show each other their discoveries, learning grows. Once they are finished, they will explain their posters to the class and state how each plant or animal on their poster is valuable to the food chain. Find a place in the classroom to display the finished products.

* Take the opportunity to ask students what role they (humans) play in the life cycles they presented; on the consuming side as well as the managing side.

Optional: If available, bring in puzzles for the students to complete in groups. Without the students knowing, remove one piece from each puzzle before giving it to them. When they are finished, discuss their feelings about missing a piece of the puzzle. Relate the missing puzzle piece to missing a piece of the food chain and discuss how that affects our environment.

Reflect: Students should reflect on their personal contributions to caring for the environment, the role they play, and the impact they have. These questions could be turned into a short writing assignment or journal entry.

Willpower

Students will better understand the value of life; it is living and giving; it is receiving and releasing. They also had an introduction to their role in protecting it and keeping it in balance.

Lesson 21

Materials

My Best Me textbook, writing utensils, journal, paper, audiovisual equipment, crayons, markers, colored pencils, construction paper for classroom rules, access to a library or Internet
* Suggestion: A great way to begin this lesson is to read the book *Berenstain Bears and the Messy Room* by Jan and Stan Berenstain. You can find a read-along version at - 4yu.info/?i=93211

Resources

Student Worksheet: 4yu.info/?i=98321
Parent Summary: 4yu.info/?i=98371

Glossary

assign, category, efficient, effective, consistent, habit, accomplish, reflect, appearance, reflection, organizational, prefer, productive

Motivation

Organization does not come naturally for everyone and is a skill that, generally, must be learned by practice to become a consistent habit. Order and structure are two essential things for accomplishing and achieving objectives in life. Let's face it, it is even a part of the hope application students are learning; setting goals, finding pathways and building willpower (this has to do with organizing). If these skills are developed and learned at an early age, it becomes part of the students' lifestyle and it will lead them to experiencing more joy and satisfaction in their life; it will allow them to be successful at whatever they put their hands to. Students can best experience this by cooperating with you as you manage the classroom. In order for a classroom to run smoothly and efficiently, rules and norms are an essential part of classroom management; it is called order, organization and structure.

When including students in the creation of rules and expectations, they are more likely to take ownership in the classroom. As they take ownership, it increases their sense of both independence and confidence.

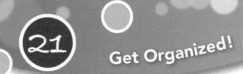

21 — Get Organized!

Goal — To understand that when I am organized my productivity increases

Pathways

Read

The library is a very special place because it contains thousands of books. Daily, people visit the library to check out many different types of texts. With so many books, how do we find what we are looking for?

Create

Assign a category to each set of books and color the books with the appropriate color.
- Red: Science fiction
- Green: Fairy tales
- Yellow: Poetry
- Purple: History
- Blue: Dictionaries

Comment

Why are libraries so orderly and organized?
What would happen if the books were not shelved in an orderly fashion?
What other places are as orderly as the library?
Have you looked for something in your bedroom and weren't able to find it?
How much time did you lose trying to find it?

Understand

Look up the words "efficient" and "effective" in the dictionary. Certainly everything works in a more efficient and effective way when we follow a certain order and maintain

---

Goal

To identify and display ways in which they can organize their school supplies, belongings and method of working and studying

Pathways

Read: Plan to take the students to the school library and have the librarian explain simply how books are categorized and organized. Once students get some insight, have them try organizing the bookshelves pictured in their textbook. Have students consider how and why the library is organized like it is.

Create: Students will use colors to organize the books on the shelves in the manner that they think works best. This gives them the opportunity to visually practice organizing a bookshelf and understand clear

a structure. An orderly and prepared place (space), a planned day (time), and a consistent habit (method) help us perform activities in an efficient way without experiencing the frustration of chaos. The way in which we maintain what surrounds us, how we organize our time and how we accomplish a task, reflect who we are. Our actions are the results of what we value. The appearance of our things is a reflection of our organizational skills. Keeping order shows that we care about ourselves and others.

 Observe

Comment

Are there differences between these two classrooms?
Describe an orderly classroom compared to one that is disorderly and disorganized. Which type of classroom do you prefer? Why?

Apply

In groups of 4, create a set of class rules that will help maintain an orderly classroom. Display rules that you will apply daily and follow in your classroom.

Reflect

How do I maintain my school supplies? My bedroom? My time? My classroom? In what ways can I improve my organizational skills?

Willpower

I organize my belongings, my time, and my method of working in order to live a more productive life.

57

---

structured systems are needed, making it easy for others to understand.

Comment: Students will be able to share their thoughts on organization with others, using the guiding questions in the workbook. Examples of other places that are structured and orderly are hospitals, supermarkets, information on line, stores, etc. Encourage your students to consider why these institutions and places are organized and structured and lead them to evaluating their own organizational routines. Which areas need improvement? Which areas can be a positive example for others? If they struggle with being organized and orderly, take time to figure out why this happens and see if students will commit to small changes in organizing and structuring their time, space and working methods.

Understand: Students will read about the importance of organizing their belongings, their time, their method of working and studying. They will also read about what effect structure and order have on

them as well as others. Of course, there will be times when they do something and things get messed up, like when they are doing an art activity. But the key is to clean things up as soon as possible, either during the time they are doing the activity or right after it is done. This process is very important for your students to recognize and understand.

Involve your students in the classroom structure and organization.

Observe/Comment: Students will observe the pictures of the orderly classroom and the messy classroom and discuss the differences. Encourage them to consider the benefits of an orderly classroom and to share how it may affect their learning and experiences.

Apply: Students will work in groups of 4 to create classroom rules and expectations. Encourage them to focus on ways to maintain an orderly classroom, rather than on behavior; however, in many instances the two will go hand in hand. Feel free to use current rules that may be posted as a guide for students to suggest changes, and allow them to add new suggestions of their own. The students' examples may be posted and then later combined to create a new, centrally located set of rules.

Reflect: Students will reflect on their own organizational skills and consider ways that they could improve. You might want to give them time to create a schedule for themselves in order to improve their time-management skills.

 **Willpower**

Students should know why order and structure is important in all that they do. It creates a way to success, satisfaction and joy.

Lesson 22

Materials

My Best Me textbook, writing utensils, journal, paper, audiovisual equipment, tape, scissors, glue, markers, pipe cleaners, reusable items: paper towel and toilet paper rolls, plastic bottles, cardboard boxes, cans, bottle caps, magazines, Popsicle sticks, fabric, yarn, etc. Ask students ahead of time to begin collecting materials and to bring them to class. Print some examples of reused materials to give students a kick start on ideas

* Suggestion: A great way to begin this lesson is to read the book *The Adventures of a Plastic Bottle* by Alison Inches and Pete Whitehead.

Resources

Student Worksheet: 4yu.info/?i=98322
Parent Summary: 4yu.info/?i=98372

Glossary

re-purpose, recycling, items, transformed, profitable, inventor,

Motivation

Reducing, reusing, and recycling are important aspects of being responsible. Accepting this responsibility will help students to be creative in finding solutions to some severe challenges to our resources. Students will understand the value of decreasing the amount of waste buried in landfills, improving the quality of our water resources and preserving all natural resources. Students will cut down on energy use and find new ways of using old items, and maybe even passing items on to others.

22 Trash or Treasure?

Goal To learn to <u>re-purpose</u> objects and materials that I no longer need

Pathways

Game

You have 3 minutes to write as many objects as you can think of that go in each trash bin. How many can you think of? Ready, set, go!!!

GLASS	PLASTIC	PAPER	METAL

_____ _____ _____ _____
_____ _____ _____ _____
_____ _____ _____ _____
_____ _____ _____ _____

Comment

Do you have any of these trash bins at your home? Which ones?
What is <u>recycling</u>? Look it up in the dictionary if you don't know.
Why would you recycle your trash?
Do you recycle at home? What gets recycled?
Name some <u>items</u> you no longer need that can be sold or reused.

Understand

There are many things we throw away because we do not like them any more, we no

Goal

To understand that many items called trash can be turned into treasures by reducing, reusing, and recycling these items

Pathways

Game: Students will race to list "trash" materials that fit under each recycling category. Once the time is up, go over their lists and evaluate their thoughts and ideas.

Comment: Students will share their experience with recycling at home and at the places they visit. Review with the students what definitions they found for recycling and discuss the other questions.

Optional: You could add to this lesson by having your students verify the amount of trash per individual in the

longer use them, or they are out of style. However, a great number of these items can be reused or <u>transformed</u> into other products that can be <u>profitable,</u> helpful, or fun to make. For example, glass bottles can be decorated and used as vases or piggy banks. Attractive jars and cardboard boxes can be creatively redesigned and used for storage. All this is possible when we are creative and motivated to start the process of reusing items that we would have otherwise thrown away. This subject also helps us think about creative solutions on how to deal with excessive amounts of trash in the environment.

Activity

What can you re-use?
Think outside the box!

Be an <u>inventor!</u> Make a treasure. Choose one trash item that you will turn into something new and try to use as many materials as possible that you would have otherwise defined as trash. Once you finish your new "invention," present it to the class.

Reflect

Do you think it is important to recycle? Why or why not?
Can you explain the title of the lesson, "Trash or Treasure"?
Did you enjoy re-purposing an item that would have otherwise been trash?
Were you able to make a treasure from trash?

I realize that trash can be treasure because many items can be transformed and reused.

59

---

inventors. The only rule is that they must use at least one recycled item or material. Be sure to ask students to bring in materials leading up to this activity and maybe even during the school year. (See materials list above.) If there are recycling bins at school, they could possibly gather materials from there and wash them out for reuse. This activity will be more fun in pairs or small groups. When their invention is complete, they will present it to the class and explain its new function/purpose.

Reflect: Students will reflect on the importance of reprocessing, especially if they change their thinking patterns toward the items they define as trash. Be sure to jump back to the title of the lesson and ask students for their thoughts on it.

The title "Trash or Treasure?" can be explained in at least three ways. One, what might seem like trash can be reused or remade into something beautiful or practical that has a new purpose, or a treasure. Two, reducing, reusing, and recycling gives us an improved environment and saves resources. Three, a new product is created that fulfills the needs and desire of consumers, for which they are willing to pay, which produces income (treasure).

---

western world; for example, the USA in comparison to the trash per individual in a developing nation, such as Haiti. If you do this activity, you can have your students research what individuals in the developing nations recycle, reuse, and reduce that results in them having such little trash. You could also have them research what kind of problems and challenges trash is creating in all the different aspects of nature.

Understand: Students will have the opportunity to brainstorm what to do with items they no longer want or need. For example, they could organize a school sale similar to a yard sale or garage sale where items are offered for sale that are no longer being used, or that have been remade into something different. They could also take items to donation centers, thrift shops, consignment stores, or other second-hand retailers. Sharing ideas and putting them into action may encourage new thoughts and behaviors.

Activity: The students will pretend to be

It is important to be able to reduce, reuse, and recycle to take care of the environment. Our environment is a treasure, and many trash items can also be transformed into treasures. It really depends upon how you look at it.

Lesson 23

Materials

My Best Me textbook, writing utensils, journal, paper, small poster for weekly care calendar, audiovisual equipment, research materials

* Suggestion: A great book you could read, *How Do Dinosaurs Love Their Cats?* by Jane Yolen and Mark Teague.

Resources

Student Worksheet: 4yu.info/?i=98323
Parent Summary: 4yu.info/?i=98373
Video: The comfort of a pet - 4yu.info/?i=93221

Glossary

mindful, mistreat, interacting, vaccinations, inspirational

Motivation

As children grow, they learn and are trained in how to properly care for themselves and become more independent. It is in those same ways that they are also able to care for and show kindness toward a pet and/or friends and family. It is important for children to understand what significance and benefit there is in caring for and serving others, and to realize the positive impact their actions can have on those around them as well as themselves.

Some students may have experience with caring for pets while others may have little to no experience, therefore working in groups would be a good option. Some students could be totally indifferent to animals and even treat them abusively due to the environments they themselves have grown up in. Therefore, going through what care looks like will help them get a better understanding.

This is one reason why it is so valuable for students to learn how to treat animals, correctly and wisely, because they are less demanding and have lower expectations. Certain character traits are required that are well learned through taking care of animals. Students will discover and consider the responsibility of having a pet, and fulfilling their needs. The same discipline they need to exercise and care for themselves is also required to care for animals.

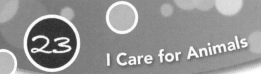

23   I Care for Animals

Goal   To learn to be <u>mindful</u> of animals and take care of them wisely

Pathways

Draw - Helping a Pet
A pet is considered healthy and happy when its needs are met. Fill in the bubbles below with what you do or can do to keep a pet healthy.

Understand
Animals are living creatures that feel (body) and have emotions (senses). They can be wild (a wolf) or tame (a pet dog). To a certain extent, they depend on us to live, whether we care for them directly or indirectly. To care for animals is to make sure that they are treated kindly, looked after, and that others don't <u>mistreat</u> or abuse them. How we treat animals is often a reflection of how we treat people.

Comment
What do pets need that people need, too?

_____

60

Goal

To understand the value of adequately caring for an animal and to list, explain and/or display how to care for animals

Pathways

Draw - Students will fill in the bubbles by writing or drawing examples of what needs to be done to care for an animal. Examples include ensuring that the pet is:

- given a name
- comfortable/has a place to sleep
- fed and has water
- not sick or injured
- given proper exercise
- loved and receives affection and attention
- clean, groomed, and free of parasites

Do I need to have traits like gentleness, patience, friendliness, etc. with a pet? What other traits are important for interacting with a pet?

Activity - Care Plan
Write a weekly plan for caring for a pet that you have (or want to have). Think about its baths, walks, food, games, rest, vaccinations, etc.

MONDAY	TUESDAY	WEDNESDAY	THURSDAY	FRIDAY	SATURDAY

Reflect
Do I have time to care for a pet? What would happen to my pet if I forgot to care for it? What would I do with my pet if I went on a trip? Can I take full responsibility for caring for a pet? Why or why not? Will I always be kind and gentle with a pet or any other animal?

Video: 4yu.info/?i=93221
Watch a wonderful inspirational clip about a boy and his puppy.

4yu.info/?i=93221

Willpower

I am mindful of my pets and other animals. I take responsibility for the care they need. It is enjoyable!

61

• up to date with its shots and injections
• safe and feels secure
• disciplined and trained correctly

Feel free to first brainstorm ideas as a class or allow children to discuss each topic in groups.

Understand: Have a student read this section aloud. It briefly addresses the responsibility involved in caring for animals. Invite students to react if they would like to opine on what they heard and thought.

Comment: Here is a chance for students to draw comparisons between caring for animals and caring for people. They can write their ideas first, then discuss as a class. Possible answers include: a need for love; food; shelter; safety; their space, etc. Different pets have different needs, which can also be discussed. Encourage students to consider all of these factors if they are ever in the position of choosing a pet for their household. Take time to cover the character traits the student themselves need to develop to properly care for an animal. The question

is even if all the above is available for an animal, what do we personally need to give and/or develop to become better at caring for animals?

Activity: A care plan for pets. Students will create a weekly plan for caring for a pet. They can choose any pet—it does not have to be a pet that they actually have. Part of the discussion can include what makes a good pet for them and their living situation (e.g., a two-bedroom apartment might not be the best place to have a hound dog). What animals are best for a family with young children? Which animals are better left in the wild? Why?

Feel free to allow students to use library resources and/or a child-friendly search engine/websites to research appropriate activities and care for the selected pet. Plans can be created in groups and/or shared with classmates and displayed upon completion. If this activity seems to be difficult for some students to do on their own, allow them to work with a partner

Reflect: Students should consider their own ability, willingness and attitude towards a pet, but even more so towards caring for that pet

Video: Attached is a very inspirational video as to how a pet can influence our life in a positive manner. It is a great way to close off the lesson - 4yu.info/?i=93221

Willpower

It is important to be able and motivated to care for pets and the animals around us. It adds responsibilities and joys to your life.

Lesson 24

Materials

My Best Me textbook, writing utensils, journal, paper, crayons, markers, or colored pencils, 8 x 8 inch pieces of a thicker paper, wooden Popsicle sticks, brass brad or pin, poster paper (optional)
* Suggestion: A great way to begin this lesson is to read the book *Why Should I Save Energy?* by Jen Green.

Resources

Student Worksheet: 4yu.info/?i=98324
Parent Summary: 4yu.info/?i=98374

Glossary

fuel, drawn, generate, renewable, energy, non-renewable, eolic energy, hydraulic energy, geothermal energy, tidal energy, conventional energy, fossil fuels, nuclear fuels, administrators, diagonal

Motivation

It can be easy to take the Earth's resources for granted and consume energy in less than responsible ways. That is why addressing this subject matter and doing it in a thought provoking manner will make the students more conscious about the decisions and actions they take. Issues like these give children insight and understanding, and motivate them to be cautious with how they use available resources. It also encourages their use of creativity to practice better habits and find new inventions that will help preserve—and even improve—the environment.

Students will know the differences between renewable and non-renewable energy, as well as discover ways in which they can conserve energy. It is our responsibility as active members of our community to understand and protect Earth's resources.

This lesson will give children insight into how some of our resources are being used. It will also provide an opportunity to brainstorm ways in which they can participate and help conserve resources with small, everyday changes in their lives.

24   Amazing Energy

Goal   To learn that there are various forms of energy in the world around me

Pathways

Read - What is Energy?

When we look around, we can see objects as well as creatures in motion. Have you ever wondered what allows them to move around? Movement is possible because of energy or <u>fuel</u>. We use energy for many things and in many different ways. Energy is <u>drawn</u> from the environment to benefit us in the things we do; for example, to <u>generate</u> electricity. Many things in our home function because of electricity. Imagine living without it! Our ancestors lived without electricity, and many people around the world still live this way. How would your life be different without electricity? Look up the word "<u>renewable</u>" in the dictionary. There are two types of <u>energy</u>, depending on its source: renewable energy and <u>non-renewable</u> energy. Renewable energy, or clean energy, is energy that comes from a never-ending source and it reproduces quickly. Examples of renewable energy include: solar energy, <u>eolic energy</u> (from the wind), <u>hydraulic energy</u> (from water), <u>geothermal energy</u> (heat from inside the earth),and <u>tidal energy</u> (from the ebb and flow of the sea). Non-renewable energy or <u>conventional</u> (common) energy, is energy that comes from a limited source, that could be used up. This is why we must think creatively about how we use energy. Examples of non-renewable energy sources include: <u>fossil fuels</u> (like coal, petroleum, and natural gas) and <u>nuclear fuels</u> (uranium and plutonium; elements found underground).

Write - Draw

Give an example of an item that is powered by each type of energy:

62

Goal

To learn the importance of energy and identify the various forms of generating energy and the pros and cons of each

Pathways

Read: Students will be introduced to two different categories of energy: renewable and non-renewable. Describe and discuss a world without electricity. What would not function in their homes if they did not have electricity? What would happen if we ran out of energy? How would our daily lives be affected?
* Consider turning off the lights, air conditioning, heater, fans, projectors, computers, etc. in the classroom for just a few minutes. How does it

Solar energy: _____

Eolic energy: _____

Hydraulic energy: _____

Geothermal energy: _____

Tidal energy: _____

Fossil fuel: _____

Nuclear fuel: _____

Understand

People have discovered and created different forms of energy from resources in our surrounding environment. We have renewable energy, which does less harm to our natural environment than non-renewable energy. As the administrators (overseers, stewards) of our natural environment, we should seek creative ways to make changes in our use of natural resources, continue to create products that improve our quality of life, and, all the time, take care of our world.

Activity - Build a windmill - Eolic energy.

Materials - 8 x 8 inch paper, 1 small wooden stick, scissors, and a brass brad or pin. Instructions:

- Fold the square paper in half.
- Fold the paper again in half. Open the paper.
- Mark the diagonal lines.
- Cut along the diagonal markings; be careful not to cut all the way to the center
- Fold each point toward the center, secure them with the brad as you pin them onto the wooden stick… let it blow!

Reflect

How can I use renewable energy in my everyday life?

Willpower

I recognize and am responsible in using the energy in the world around me. 🙂

63

---

it implies to administer the available resources and invite students to share their thoughts on this issue.

Activity: Students will be creating their own paper windmill to explore eolic energy (derived from the wind). Read aloud the instructions on how to make this windmill. You might demonstrate the "how to" if you think your students need that help. Allow students to work in pairs or small groups for collaboration. Give students the opportunity to explore their windmill both inside and outside, and observe how the windmill functions in different environments.

*Suggestion: you can also have students decorate their windmills.

*Suggestion: you can also have students make different sizes of windmills.

Reflect: Students will be able to reflect on what they have learned about various types of energy. Students can discuss this topic or respond to it in writing.

---

feel? This could also be done as a warm-up at the beginning of the lesson before reading. It might also be interesting to mention things like running water, stoplights, metro or subway, phone services, cars functioning, etc. A lot can go wrong when energy is not generated!

Evaluate students' understanding of the reading and ask if they have any questions or thoughts.

Write/Draw: Give the students the option of writing a description, giving an example, or drawing an example of each type of energy. You may want to provide them with the information or have them research on their own. Students could also be divided into pairs or groups and assigned one type of energy to research. They could also make a poster or find video clips or images on-line to present their findings to the class.

Understand: Give students time to read this section and allow them to make observations and remarks about what they read. Focus on what

Willpower

It is important for the student to understand that we (humans) are the key to conserving Earth's natural resources; inventing new energy sources and motivating others to participate in safeguarding our planet for ourselves, our children and grandchildren.

Lesson 25

Materials
My Best Me textbook, writing utensils, journal, paper, notebook/science journal for recording notes, tomato seeds, small cups, cotton balls
* Suggestion: A great way to begin this lesson is to read the book *From Seed to Plant* by Gail Gibbons.

Resources
Student Worksheet: 4yu.info/?i=98325
Parent Summary: 4yu.info/?i=98375

Glossary
planet, sceneries, climates, requires, determine, rechargeable,

Motivation
Most of us tend to take nature and planet Earth for granted. It is easy to enjoy nature, the environment, and the resources available to us, but it really comes with great responsibility and duty. Students will understand that resources are like treasures that we should learn to value and cherish. We should not only desire to live in a world that is clean and aesthetically pleasing, but desire the same for our great grandchildren. That is possible if everyone does their part by learning to be responsible, respectful, and mindful of the environment and the needs of Earth itself.

Of course, we cannot underestimate the new inventions and discoveries our children and their children's children will come up with that will deal with some of the challenging issues Earth faces. Nevertheless, children and adults alike can benefit from learning ways they can care for the Earth and manage it so it can continue to produce its designed abundance. One simple and very impactful way to do this is through planting plants; especially trees.

25 The World Around Me

Goal
To learn how to protect and improve my natural environment

Pathways

Read
Planet Earth is a gift to us. Its beautiful sceneries, valuable resources, different climates and all the creatures living in it exist for us to enjoy and appreciate. It provides richly for our daily needs. Like any other gift, it requires maintenance (care, attention), even more so because it sustains our lives. If we are not respectful of our environment, tending to its needs, and generous in sharing what it yields, we will lose nature's beauty as we know it, and will endanger our own survival.

Our daily actions affect the planet and its natural resources in a positive or negative way and determine the health of our planet. Take a moment to consider how your actions affect your environment.

Understand
Is the following helpful or harmful? Draw a happy face if the action helps the environment, or a sad face if it harms the environment.
- Throw garbage in its proper place.
- Plant a tree with my family.
- Leave the lights on at home.
- Turn the television off when I am not using it.
- Choose products that can be reused or recycled.
- Use rechargeable batteries.
- Let the water run while I brush my teeth.

64

Goal

Identify creative ways through which they can protect and promote the mindful care of the environment

Pathways

Read: By reading this section, students will begin to consider how the Earth is a gift and why. Earth is alive and has a life of its own. We are called to manage it, care for it and structure it to produce sustainably for all its habitants. If we do that, Earth will continue to provide for us abundantly.

Telling students what they should appreciate and do (and not do) to care for the environment is good, but, it is far more valuable to lead them into a discovery of the environment and where they fit so they can understand and appreciate the many things

Write - Draw

Think of one other positive action that you can take to benefit the environment. Draw a picture of the action and write two sentences to explain how it helps the environment.

_____
_____
_____
_____
_____
_____
_____

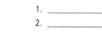

Apply - make a difference, plant tomatoes!

- Place a tomato seed between two pieces of cotton.
- Wet the cotton with water.
- Place it inside a small cup.
- Repeat the process with a bean.
- Place one cup in the sun and the other in the shade.
- Each day, observe what happens in each cup.

Reflect

How does planting seeds make a difference to the environment? What are some actions you do that could be hurting the environment? How can you change them? Make two commitments/goals that will help your take better care of the Earth.

1. _____
2. _____

Willpower

I am committed to protecting and improving my environment to the best of my ability.

65

---

they encounter in life. In this discovery, there is a greater chance of them becoming owners of their observations and insights. This will then guide them into making better and wiser decisions. As educators, it is our task to present these subjects in an attractive way so we pique their interest and desire to seek and find solutions.

Understand: Students will identify helpful or harmful actions to the environment by drawing a happy or sad face behind each sentence. After discussing their answers and students defending their view points, have students brainstorm other ways in which they can help the environment.

Draw: Students will think of one more positive action they can undertake to help the environment. Once they have thought of one action they will draw that action or one of the prior ones from the list. In the space below, they will then explain what is happening in their picture to help the environment and what is their responsibility.

Apply: Students will be given the opportunity to observe the life cycle of a tomato seed. Use a notebook or science journal to allow them to compare the seed's growth in and out of sunlight. After daily observation for about 2 weeks, discuss the difference in growth between the seed in the sun and the seed in the shade. The sun affects the seed just as we affect our environment.

You could also discuss the idea that our environment affects our ability to grow, as well. For example, we also need clean water, fresh air, and sunlight to grow. Encourage students to plant the seed at home or in a school garden, as this is one more way to make a positive impact on the environment and learn what happens when you seize the initiative and take action.

Reflect: Students will reflect on their experience and research by answering the questions and committing to two positive actions they will take to protect and improve the environment. If possible, see if there are any community projects, such as a park clean-up, or school fix-up that could be arranged.

Willpower

It is important that students understand that Earth is our home and, therefore, it is our responsibility to keep Earth a wonderful and safe place to live.

Lesson 26

Materials

My Best Me textbook, writing utensils, journal, paper, colored pencils (optional)
* Suggestion: A great way to begin this lesson is to read the book *Rich Man Poor Man* by J.R. Poulter or *Mr. King's Things* by Genevieve Cote.

Resources

<u>Student Worksheet:</u> 4yu.info/?i=98326
<u>Parent Summary:</u> 4yu.info/?i=98376

Glossary

prized, possessions, external, disaster, access, extend, deserted,

Motivation

Many of us get caught up chasing after material possessions, with a tendency to think our goods determine our worth and success. It is, therefore, no wonder our children are similarly absorbed with material things such as toys, electronics, candy, fancy clothes, and always wanting more of everything. They learn from us! Let's face it; as the adults who influence our children, sometimes we do not set the best example in valuing the invaluable things around us.

Advertisers are very clever at targeting children, especially as they promote the false belief that only through possessing their item can happiness be experienced. Their focus is also directed to busy parents, suggesting that they can compensate for decreased quality time with their children by buying them the newest gadgets. Thus, it perpetuates the false impression that the gadget is equal to spending time together, and justifies the purchase. When we get caught up in this rat race, the danger is that we can lose our appreciation for the truly valuable things in life.

Prized Possessions

Goal To understand what is truly important in my life

Pathways

 Activity - "Let's go!"
Imagine you will be taking a journey to a deserted island. You will stay on the island for three months. The only food available on the island is fish and coconuts. Decide what you will take with you on your trip. What can't you live without? Draw or write down the items in your suitcase.

 Comment
Do you consider the things you chose as your most <u>prized</u> <u>possessions</u>? Why?
What is missing in your suitcase to have an unforgettable trip?
What or who is important to you that cannot be placed in a suitcase?
Are these people or things more important than what goes into your suitcase?

 Understand
There are material items that we value very much (things like toys, game consoles, bikes, etc.). We even think we cannot live without them. Did you think about the people in your life when you made the list above? We all enjoy the phone we use, the clothes we wear, the car our family drives, the house we live in and the money we spend, but these <u>external</u> material things can be taken away from us at any time. And then what? We will discover that the really important things; the things we truly cannot live without are the people we interact with and love.

68

 Goal

To recognize the true treasures and possessions of life and value and appreciate them accordingly

 **Pathways**

Activity: Students will brainstorm the most important items they would pack in a suitcase for a long vacation. They will draw or write the items in their suitcase. Have the students focus on why these things are so important to them and how/why they would need them on the deserted island.

Most students will need a change in their mindset to help them realize that the most important things in life are actually not objects. The things that bring us joy come from our relationships with friends and family, the experiences, journeys and memories we build with them,

62

The true wealth of every nation is in its people. When a country or a city experiences a <u>disaster</u>, people may not have <u>access</u> to their cars, possessions, or homes. Very often, the only thing left are other people around them who <u>extend</u> their hands and their care, who share what they have and help to rebuild what was lost.

On a <u>deserted</u> island we would discover that our true treasures are not the material items we tend to value so much, but the people we have in our lives.

Write

Who are the important people in your life?

Think of three people (or relationships) you have that are of great value to you. Write each one on the line and explain why each one is valuable to you.

1. _____: _____
   _____
   _____: _____
   _____
2. _____: _____
   _____

Reflect

When I value something or someone, how do I demonstrate that?

Do I tell the people who are important to me that I value them? How?

What are some ways to show others (through actions) that I hold them dear?

What is a valuable moment or experience you shared with your family?

What do I value about myself?

How do I demonstrate to friends and family that I value myself?

Willpower

The relationships I have with people are the most important possessions I have.

---

a discovery process about why certain things seem to be so important. (No one should feel the need to defend themselves.)

Understand: The reading gives students the chance to consider what the words "rich" and "valuable" really mean, and to think about what their lives would look like without the precious relationships and experiences they have with family and friends. As you or your students read this section aloud, stop intermittently to digest and discuss what was written and what their thoughts are.

Write: Students will choose three people, places, or things that hold great value for them, and explain why they are valuable. If they choose a material item, be sure they are choosing it for sentimental reasons, not for monetary value (have them try to forget about their phone.) You may want to have a discussion about the meaning of "sentimental value." Encourage them to consider nature, experiences, relationships, and even activities: a beautiful view; swimming in the ocean; looking at the stars; etc.

Reflect: Students will have the opportunity to respond to the following workbook questions regarding the lesson activities. Since this topic may provoke quite a bit of self-reflection and deep thought, allow students to respond in the way they feel most comfortable (e.g., privately in their journal or workbook, with a partner, etc.).

and our ability to help each other and share life together.

Other things that are of great value and that can bring great joy are focusing on the dreams and ideas within us, and allowing them to become reality by making plans and developing them.

This lesson is for students to learn to navigate some of the "consumerism" pressures society puts on them and to learn to have more fun with less "stuff." The goal is to help them refocus their sincere appreciation for the people they care about in their everyday lives, for the adventures, memories and experiences shared, for the opportunities and journeys traveled, for the pursuit and fulfilling of dreams, and for the building of meaning and significance in their lives.

Comment: Students will have the opportunity to comment on what they would take on their trip, using the workbook questions provided. Give them time to share their answers with a classmate, as well as question their classmates on why they would take certain items. Be sure to guide the exercise so it is

Willpower

The most prized possessions are relationships and these are generally tied to experiences or significant moments that create memories and bonding. Be sensitive to the fact that some of your students may have lost valuable relationships due to death, divorce, relocation, etc.

Lesson 27

Materials

My Best Me textbook, writing utensils, journal, paper, crayons, markers, colored pencils

*Suggestion: A great way to begin this lesson is to read the book *The Leaf That Wouldn't Change* by Whitney Bitner.

Resources

Student Worksheet: 4yu.info/?i=98327
Parent Summary: 4yu.info/?i=98377
Template Circle: 4yu.info/?i=93271

Glossary

identical, original, authentic

Motivation

Being unique and special is a positive part of everyday life. As we relate with each other and work together, we come to realize that it is our differences that allow us to create so many amazing and awesome things in this world, and to enjoy and use them for our benefit.

Young children have the wonderful ability to embrace and accept others for who they are. The differences and diversities are not really taken into consideration by them, but absorbed as part of the whole picture. However, as children grow older, they tend to become more judgmental and critical, and they start experiencing the pressure to fit in and avoid being different or unique. These gradual changes can make it increasingly difficult for children to feel free to be exactly who they are, or to do the things they are good at.

There is great value in teaching students to continue to operate in the same openness of their early childhood; to embrace others as well as their own unique qualities and differences. Students who learn to accept themselves at a young age, and are comfortable and confident with who they are, set a great example for their peers. Such students will create a safe space and the liberty for others their age to be themselves. Teaching children the value of being different and accepting themselves will also help them develop a joy of living authentic lives and accepting others for who they are.

27 — World's #1 Resource: People

Goal To understand the value of others

Pathways

Observe

At first glance you will see two drawings that seem to be <u>identical</u>, but after looking carefully you will be able to find seven differences between the drawings. Can you find them?

Comment

Was it difficult to find the differences?
Did you enjoy finding the differences and similarities?
Think about the people in your life—their differences and similarities.
What would life be like if we were all the same in every possible way?
What are some benefits of being different and unique?
See if you can list at least 3 benefits.

1. _____
2. _____
3. _____

Understand

People are the most important aspect of our life. The better we understand this, the greater our relationships can become, because we learn to value each and every one for who they are. Each person is different physically, mentally, emotionally, and

Goal

To recognize and embrace the benefits and joy of being unique and different, in others as well as in themselves

Pathways

Observe: Students will have the opportunity to identify similarities and differences in the two drawings side by side. Some differences may be easy to locate, while others will take more time. This activity can be used to demonstrate that while some characteristics of people may be the same, others may not. These characteristics may be quick to observe, while others are revealed to us as we get to know one another. You could enhance this activity by asking students to name some similarities and differences among themselves. It is part of life and students

spiritually. Even identical twins are very different from each other and hold their own identities. How we are designed makes us special and unique. Our different gifts and talents give us the opportunity to share ourselves in our own unique way with others around us. These are the qualities that make us who we are. It is amazing how each person can dream, invent, and create things in special ways that positively impact their surrounding world.

 Create
What do you imagine the circle could be?
Use your creativity to use or decorate it.

 Comment
Compare your circle design with those of your classmates. Did anyone do the same thing with the circle?
What are your thoughts on the different circle art works your class produced?
Why does your design look different from your classmates' designs? Did any of the other designs come close to what you created?
Do you prefer some circle art more than others? Why?
If each person's circle was put on display in your classroom, would they be interesting to look at if all of them were exactly the same?

 Reflect
Name at least two ways in which you are creative, unique and special.
How do these characteristics impact the people around you?
Is it hard to be <u>original</u>? Why?
Do you fear being unique and different? Why?

Everyone is <u>authentic</u> and unique, and that makes life interesting.

71

---

should be comfortable talking about their observations because it helps break down the bias that hides away in each of us.

 Comment: Students will have the opportunity to answer the questions in writing or in discussion format. This topic may be sensitive to students who have a difficult time fitting in or who lack the confidence to show exactly who they are. Create a safe environment for students who wish to share both positive and negative personal experiences of being unique, while also having the ability to make personal connections with classmates.

Understand: Students should realize that people are the most important resource in their lives; their creativity, abilities, mannerisms, knowledge and wisdom are means (or tools) that can enhance our lives as well as the lives of others. Have students read this section aloud and evaluate their thoughts on what was read.

Create: Without any specific instructions, have students create anything they imagine or want in or around the empty circle on the page. You could also have identical cut out paper circles ready to go for students to decorate as they desire - 4yu.info/?i=93271 Now they have a specific opportunity to show themselves and others who they are by their unique and particular way of filling in or decorating the circle. Remember to let them be creative; some might want to draw outside of the circle.

A suggestion: Make a photo of each circle art work and then print them out and hang them around the classroom for each student to observe. This will remind them how valuable it is to be different and unique.

Comment: Students will have the opportunity to comment on their drawing with a partner and answer the provided questions.

* Suggestion: Share Something Positive (this activity is not in the workbook): Have each student write their name at the top of a piece of paper. The paper will then be passed around to every student. Each student will have a few seconds to write down one positive comment about the classmate whose name is at the top of the page. Give the students a few seconds for each piece of paper before moving it to the next student. At the end of the activity, all the students will have a list of positive comments/traits about themselves.

Reflect: Students can reflect on today's lesson in writing or in discussion format.

It is important to understand that being unique and different is a very positive part of life. Our differences help us create greatness and beauty.

Lesson 28

Materials

My Best Me textbook, writing utensils, journal, crayons, markers, colored pencils, paper to create a daily or weekly schedule
* Suggestion: A great way to begin this lesson is to read the book *Amanda and the Lost Time* by Shelley Admont.

Resources

Student Worksheet: 4yu.info/?i=98328
Parent Summary: 4yu.info/?i=98378
Template Schedule: 4yu.info/?i=93281

Glossary

scheduled, regardless, background, origin, manage, define, unreachable, tasks, pattern, prioritize

Motivation

Time management can only be successful if your students have a concept of what time means. It is an element of life that is constant and changing continually. Some days fly by like a breath of fresh air, while others seem to drag on forever. We all have the same portion of this non-renewable resource. How do we help students understand the concept of time and grasp its great value, maximizing this resource to its full benefit?

Time management is a skill that is necessary to navigate the everyday rigors of life, and invaluable for students to learn and develop at the earliest juncture. The use of time reflects what is important to an individual. Talk to students about their perception of the duration of time and events, and the sequence of activities during a school day. Make comparisons between one day and another, referring to the past, present, and future, as you emphasize activities related to time. Examples of comparison could be: how much do they accomplish on the day before they travel or what happens on first day after school is over?

28 Structuring Time

Goal To learn to <u>maximize</u> my time

Pathways

Draw

<u>Mingle!</u> Find different students who fit each statement and write their names on the lines.

1. _____ wakes up at 6:00 am.
2. _____ wakes up earlier than 6:00 am.
3. _____ wakes up later than 6:00 am.
4. _____ eats dinner at 5:00 pm.
5. _____ eats dinner at 6:00 pm.
6. _____ goes to bed before 8:00 pm.
7. _____ goes to bed after 9:00 pm.
8. _____ does their homework before dinner.
9. _____ does their homework after dinner.
10. _____ helps with chores after school.

 Comment

Do you eat your meals at the same time each day?
Do you wake up and go to bed at the same time each day?
Do you have a <u>scheduled</u> time each day to do your homework?
To exercise? To play with friends? To help with chores?
What things do you spend most of your day doing?
Is it important to have a schedule for all of your activities? Why?

 Understand

Time is a valuable non-renewable resource. As the hours, minutes, and seconds pass, we can never again regain them. All people, <u>regardless</u> of social class, <u>background</u>, or <u>origin</u>, count on the same measure of time. However, there is a great difference between

72

 Goal

To better develop their time concept; learn to value time and discover how to manage time wisely

 **Pathways**

Draw: Before you start the lesson, ask students to describe the word "time" to you. This will cause them to focus. Have students "mingle" to learn about each other's daily routines through the given questions. Be sure they write a different student's name on each blank (10). This will ensure that everyone participates, plus it's more fun to get up and walk around! They will also discover how time is used in different ways.

 Comment: Have students answer these

what people accomplish within the same amount of time. Consistently scheduling your time and activities will help you <u>manage</u> your time in the best way possible. As you do, you will discover that you can get far more done than you thought! Making daily, weekly, monthly and yearly plans and schedules about the goals you want to achieve helps you <u>define</u> how and what needs to happen, and when it would be best to do so. It also breaks down what might seem to be <u>unreachable</u> goals into smaller steps that can be accomplished. Writing these goals and steps down will cause you to focus, give you clarity, save you time and put your <u>tasks</u> in order, from the most important to the least important. If you develop this habit and follow this <u>pattern</u>, you will have time to create, work, play, and rest.

Activity

Simon and Allen go to school until 2:00 pm. After school, they participate in sports until 3:30 pm. They also have to do chores and do their homework, all before dinner at 6:30 pm.

Simon's Chores:
- Sweep the kitchen floor.
- Take out the trash.
- Walk the dog.

Allen's Chores:
- Water the flowers.
- Fold your clothes.
- Empty the dishwasher.

Help Simon and Allen organize their schedules so they can accomplish their chores in time.

Simon		Allen	
Time	Activity	Time	Activity

Reflect

Make a weekly schedule for yourself of all the daily activities you take part in.

Willpower

I organize my time, <u>prioritize</u> my activities, and <u>evaluate</u> the results on a daily basis. 🙂

73

questions individually, then as a class discussion. The goal is to engage students' thinking in the concept of a healthy, productive daily routine as they compare their routines with one another.

Understand: Some of the most successful students (and adults) are those who have learned to use their time wisely, at an early age and found a healthy balance between work and play. One powerful tool they use is writing out a plan where activities are tied to time, through which they accomplished the goals they have set using a step-by-step process.

Third grade students are at an age that they can understand the precious resource that is time. Help them think pro-actively about how they use their time each day. If they can grasp this simple concept of the incredible value of time, and begin to appreciate it now and learn how to use and mange it in a productive way, they will have a head start in life.

Activity: Students learn best through structure, which may include schedules, routines, and explicit

teaching and practice of prioritizing activities and creating and editing schedules.

They will help prioritize and organize Simon and Allen's schedule listed in the workbook. Remind them to include a starting and ending time for each activity. Before the students start this activity, one idea is to help them calculate how much time each chore will take. This is a good opportunity to develop insight into their concept of time. Some students will be better at this than others, so use them to explain it to their peers. Once the time estimate is finished for each chore, have the students develop a schedule.

 Reflect: Students will also be able to organize their day or week in a schedule format. (You may decide to do it in steps and allow them to create a schedule one day at a time, helping them develop a better sense of time until they have completed the whole week.) The first step is to define all their activities. Then students will need time to research their own formats for organizing a daily or weekly schedule. It could be that they create their own template, or look for a printable/editable schedule available for free use on the Internet. Encourage students to share and use their schedule as part of a new routine. You might also have a template available if this becomes too time consuming (see resources) - 4yu.info/?i=93281. Remember that it is not about them finding a good schedule; rather, it is about them learning to fill in and follow a schedule. It would also be beneficial for students to revisit their schedule format after some time to make changes if necessary.

Willpower

Students will have a better concept of time and are developing their ability to manage their time on a daily basis in a healthy manner.

Lesson 29

Materials
My Best Me textbook, writing utensils, journal, crayons, markers, colored pencils, paper objects from around the classroom
* Suggestion: A great way to begin this lesson is to read the book *Prudy's Problem and How She Solved It* by Carey Armstrong-Ellis. Have students read aloud, or you may choose to read the book to the students.

Resources
Student Worksheet: 4yu.info/?i=98329
Parent Summary: 4yu.info/?i=98379

Glossary
brute, projectile, entrepreneur, farmhand, Drummond, poeticized, obstacle, hurdles, opportunities, viewpoint

Motivation
   Obstacles and unpleasant situations in life are inevitable and can be hard on one's emotional state of being. It is important for students to learn that the way they view, approach, and handle any situation will greatly determine its outcome. Problem-solving skills and creative thinking are crucial in and out of the classroom. Help students understand that they can bring about change for better by changing their perception of the obstacle and their attitude toward it. The best way they can make constructive changes is to create an environment where they consistently surround themselves with people and things that are supportive of their goals.

   In today's lesson, students will be able to brainstorm extraordinary ways to use everyday objects, compelling them to view situations, things, and people differently. They will work together with their peers to see things from another's perspective and open their minds to new possibilities. At the same time, they will be presented with a wide range of thoughts and opinions.

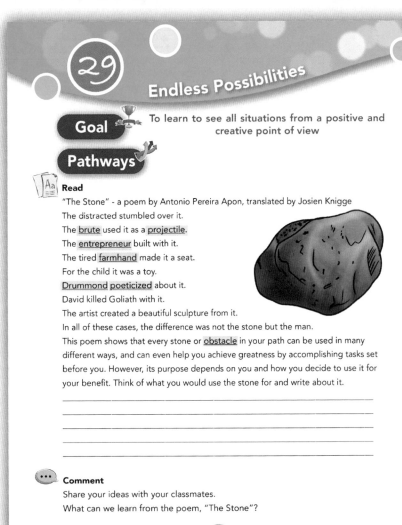

Goal
To learn to see all situations from a positive and creative point of view

Pathways

Read
"The Stone" - a poem by Antonio Pereira Apon, translated by Josien Knigge
The distracted stumbled over it.
The brute used it as a projectile.
The entrepreneur built with it.
The tired farmhand made it a seat.
For the child it was a toy.
Drummond poeticized about it.
David killed Goliath with it.
The artist created a beautiful sculpture from it.
In all of these cases, the difference was not the stone but the man.
This poem shows that every stone or obstacle in your path can be used in many different ways, and can even help you achieve greatness by accomplishing tasks set before you. However, its purpose depends on you and how you decide to use it for your benefit. Think of what you would use the stone for and write about it.

_____
_____
_____
_____
_____

Comment
Share your ideas with your classmates.
What can we learn from the poem, "The Stone"?

74

Goal

To understand that how you view, approach and tackle a situation, especially difficult ones, will affect its outcome

Pathways

   Read and Write: The students will read the poem called "The Stone," by Antonio Pereira Apon. Through creative thinking, the writer describes different and unexpected applications of a simple stone (a hard thing in life). Help your students see that even something as ordinary as a rock (an obstacle) can be transformed into something exceptional and useful, or something destructive and damaging. After reading the poem, there is space for students to write and add their own ideas for other uses of the stone that have not yet been mentioned. Encourage the

Understand

Every day we will find obstacles in our way. These hurdles provide opportunities to create and invent new things or learn more about ourselves and our environment. However, our success in overcoming these hurdles is determined by our attitude and creativity. If we practice looking at hurdles and things that frustrate us from a different viewpoint, they just might turn out to be a key to our success and future. Our point of view can and will change the outcome of a situation!

Create

Pretend to be inventors in the "Land of the Alternate Inventions"

- Form groups of 3 people.
- Imagine you live in a land of inventors; everyone invents something, and everything that is invented is accepted by everyone else.
- Each group chooses an object and invents new ways to use it.
- The group that gives the greatest varieties of uses to the chosen object, wins.
- The object your group chose was:

____

The new uses that were given to this object are:

____

____

Reflect

How do I react in my daily life when I face an obstacle?
Do I look at these difficult situations in a positive way?
Do I try to use all of life's events in a positive manner? How?
If not, how can I change that?

Willpower

I take advantage of every obstacle and challenge because I know it is an opportunity to learn and grow.

students to think outside of the box. (Some other ideas: decoration for fish tank, a paper weight, a road block, a "pet" rock, a water purifying/restructuring system, etc.)

Comment: Students will share with the class their own ideas about other uses for a stone. Make sure students understand that none of their thoughts or ideas are out of order or weird. Let's face it, who would have thought stone is used to guard written files on a USB drive, which are made out of stone! The liberty to think completely out of the box, because when there is no judgement or critique it can result in amazing discoveries and ideas, which is your goal for the classroom as the teacher. Encourage a discussion about what can be learned from the poem.

Understand: As they read, students will see the relationship between the stone in the poem and their perception of hard and difficult life situations from different perspectives. Allow students to share their thoughts on how a stone can be compared with the hardships of life. Help students understand these difficult situations in their life can all be approached creatively when they maintain a positive attitude. These obstacles and hardships that we encounter in life can make us better individuals or we can allow them to make us worse. We make that decision; not the obstacles.

Create: A moment of "crazy thinking;" nothing will be too weird or silly nothing is impossible, nothing is too expensive! In today's activity, students will form groups of 3 and use an ordinary object in the classroom (or another everyday object from home) and brainstorm various different uses for it. This activity will help the group think creatively, pull them out of tradition and promote discussion about the object. The students will make a list in their workbook and can add descriptions as well. Once they have done so, they can present their ideas to the class. Allow the class to spontaneously add on other uses as the groups present their objects. Use the white board or another medium to capture the different usage ideas.

Reflect: Students may use the provided workbook questions to guide them in today's reflection on looking at situations from various perspectives.

Willpower

Students understand that a positive perspective changes the outcome of any situation. Also, hardships in life really are key to making us stronger and helping us form our character.

Lesson 30

Materials
My Best Me textbook, writing utensils, journal, paper
* Suggestion: A great way to begin this lesson is to read the book *Dreams Come True ... All They Need is You!* by Mike Dooley.

Resources
Student Worksheet: 4yu.info/?i=98330
Parent Summary: 4yu.info/?i=98380

Glossary
entire, impassable, barrier, milkweed, astonishment, antennae, emerge, Monarc butterfly, encounter, achieve, persevere

Motivation
We all long for a sense of belonging, purpose, and the feeling that we are moving forward. Our dreams are a key factor in reaching our destiny and climbing to great heights. Dreams truly are the substance and foundation of what is yet to come into existence; nothing around us would have its existence without having first been a dream, thought, or idea. When we dream to do something or be someone, we have something to look forward to and strive for. We put the images and ideas of our mind into words, then we design what we saw and create it to be used by others or ourselves. These dreams and goals give us direction to become better, see further, and expand our influence. This is what hope is all about; putting those dreams into goals, finding the pathways to achieve the set goals and building willpower to make it happen.

Even if we briefly lose our way with life's everyday distractions, our dreams and goals remind us to re-focus and get back on track. When we achieve our dreams and reach our goals, we pull the intangible realm into the tangible world; we feel a sense of dignity and accomplishment. This accomplishment gives us satisfaction, knowing that we've worked hard and are capable of so much.

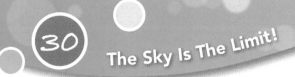

30 The Sky Is The Limit!

Goal To learn that there are no limits to accomplishing my dreams

Pathways

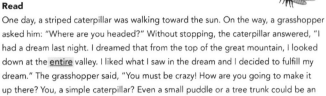

Read

One day, a striped caterpillar was walking toward the sun. On the way, a grasshopper asked him: "Where are you headed?" Without stopping, the caterpillar answered, "I had a dream last night. I dreamed that from the top of the great mountain, I looked down at the <u>entire</u> valley. I liked what I saw in the dream and I decided to fulfill my dream." The grasshopper said, "You must be crazy! How are you going to make it up there? You, a simple caterpillar? Even a small puddle or a tree trunk could be an <u>impassable</u> <u>barrier</u> to you." But the caterpillar kept moving and was determined not to let the grasshopper discourage him. The spider, the mole, and the frog all told him it was impossible. But nothing stopped the caterpillar.

A little tired, the caterpillar decided to rest for a while. "I will accomplish my dream, but I must first stop to rest," was the last thing the caterpillar said before he laid down to sleep. As time went on, the animals realized that the caterpillar was nowhere to be found. They feared something terrible had happened to him on his journey. Then one morning, when the sun shone bright in the sky, the animals received news of something unusual happening just outside of town.

They all rushed to the large <u>milkweed</u> bush just outside the village limits, and were amazed at what they saw. There hung a hard green shell, which began to break. With great <u>astonishment</u>, they saw eyes and <u>antennae</u> <u>emerge</u> that couldn't possibly belong to a caterpillar. Little by little, the beautiful wings of a butterfly fluttered out from its shell. Indeed, the caterpillar had transformed into a strong <u>monarch butterfly</u> and now would be able to accomplish his dream of flying to the top of the mountain!

76

Goal

To realize that their dreams (the intangible realm of thoughts and imagination) are valuable and can be accomplished with determination and creativity

Pathways

Read: The students will have the opportunity to hear about a caterpillar who has big dreams that others don't believe he can achieve. Let's face it, they do seem impossible for the caterpillar. However, when the caterpillar transforms into a butterfly, he is able to reach the goal he set in his mind. He also proves that no outside influence stood in his way. The caterpillar grew and matured into a creature that was able to accomplish his dreams. We should be inspired to grow, change and transform to be people who reach the heights we set for ourselves. We might not be able to

Comment

What was the caterpillar's dream?

Did the caterpillar <u>encounter</u> obstacles? What were they?

What did the other animals think of the caterpillar's dream?

Do you have a dream that you haven't shared with anyone?

Understand

Each of us has been given a unique mind that allows us to dream, and we also have the drive to accomplish these dreams. Nothing and no one can stop us from accomplishing our dreams if we truly believe we can achieve them. Our confidence in ourselves must be greater than the negative advice of the people around us or the barriers in life that will try to stop us. We just need to use our creativity and determination until we accomplish our goal.

Activity

Think about your dreams and goals while you complete the following sentences.

My dream is _____

What can stop me from living my dream is _____

I am not limited to _____

I have _____

I can accomplish _____

I will <u>achieve</u> _____

"<u>Persevere</u>" means _____

Reflect

Take a moment to think about your dreams. What is your purpose in life?

How do you plan on accomplishing your dreams?

Name three things you will need in order to achieve your dreams? Why?

Willpower

I know that I am able and capable of accomplishing my dreams.

77

---

do certain things now, but that's what goals are for.

 Comment: Create a classroom discussion guided by the provided questions. Encourage the students to make real-life connections of their own to the story. Give students the opportunity to journal about their personal dreams and aspirations instead of sharing with others. Remind them that by just writing down their dreams, the chances of them becoming a reality in their life increases by almost 50%.

Understand: This is a prime opportunity to help your students understand the precious value of their dreams and goals. Life can be difficult and comes with a lot of responsibilities; adults understand this. Some of your students might have already experienced severe hardship or major disappointment, while other students may not have yet experienced any difficulties. Nevertheless, all of your students will have dreams, that might be hidden deep within them. These are the worlds to be, the possibilities for making things better. Do all you can to invite them to

put words to those dreams; allow them to dare to imagine these dreams becoming reality. Pull your students toward greatness by having them meditate on those dreams and how they can become reality. As you instill in them the value, importance, and authenticity of their dreams, it will help establish a foundation upon which they can build in the future.

Activity: Students will complete the sentence starters regarding a specific dream that each student identifies. Allow students to research "perseverance" and to discuss what the word means to them. Some of the questions might seem vague; nevertheless, continue to direct their attention to what it would take to accomplish their dreams (what that requires and looks like). You can help by having them look up people they admire, and reading their biography. What did this individual do, encounter, sacrifice, and think to reach their dream?

The most incredible treasures are buried in graveyards; that is where unwritten songs, books and poems were silenced forever, just like new inventions and medical cures. Therefore, it is critical that we stir up the dreams in our students and encourage them to live up to their full potential; they just have to want it!

Reflect: Students will think about their own dreams. Encourage them to write about their current goals and develop a plan that will help them turn their dreams into reality.

Willpower

It is important to understand that having unique dreams and aspirations makes life more meaningful. Hope is the power to accomplish them by setting goals, finding pathways and developing willpower. They can do anything they decide to do!

Glossary

Access: freedom to make use of something (#69)

Accompany: go with (#47)

Accomplish: bring to completion (#57)

Achieve: to carry out with success (#77)

Adequate: enough to meet the need (#55)

Administrators: people in a management role (#63)

Adolescence: stage of human development in ages 10-19 (#18)

Adopted: taken in as part of a family (#40)

Affection: feelings of love or devotion (#28)

Affects: produces a change in; impact felt (#16) (#26)

Affirmative: encouraging; positive (#41)

Amazed: great wonder or surprise (#36)

Antennae: a pair of slender, movable organs on the heads of insects (#76)

Anxious: fearful; strong pressure (#48)

Appearance: the way something or someone looks (#57)

Appears: looks like (#34)

Ashamed: feeling of guilt or embarrassment (#47)

Assign: to delegate a task (#56)

Astonishment: great surprise; wonder; amazement (#76)

Attention: applying your thoughts to something or someone (#21)

Attentively: act of focusing your thoughts on (#42)

Attitude: a feeling or emotion towards something (#22)

Authentic: being exactly as it appears (#71)

Background: place time and setting when something occurs (#72)

Balanced: having different parts properly arranged (#27)

Bandanna: a large colorful handkerchief (#14)

Barrier: something that blocks passage (#76)

Behavior: the manner of conducting oneself (#16)

Bond: a coming together or binding (#13)

Boundaries: limits to how far something can go (#20)

Brute: of animal quality or harsh (#74)

Capable: showing general ability (#46)

Carved: cut with care and precision (#22)

Category: a basic division or grouping of things (#56)

Caterpillar: the worm-like insect that transforms to a butterfly or moth (#54)

Challenges: difficult tasks or problems (#32)

Characteristics: special qualities or appearances in an individual (#18)

Circumstances: events that affect a situation (#36)

Climates: the average weather conditions of a place (#64)

Common: used frequently; not unusual (#12)

Compare: to examine for similarity or differences (#13)

Compassion: pity for and a desire to help someone (#45)

Complex: not easy to understand (#28) (#55)

Compliments: best wishes of respect and admiration (#28)

Condition: to change the habits of usually by training (#34)

Confident: certain about your ability to do things well (#21)

Confidentiality: to keep other people's information secret (#11)

Conflicts: extended struggles (#49)

Consequences: the effects following bad decisions (#27)

Consider: to think about carefully (#14)

Considerate: thoughtful of the rights and feelings of others (#42)

Consistent: always the same (#57)

Content: pleased and satisfied; not needing more (#30)

Conventional: following the usual or accepted way of doing things (#62)

Conversation: a talk between two or more people (#27)

Corresponding: having qualities in common (#50)

Courage: strength of heart to carry on even in danger (#21)

Courteous: showing consideration and good manners (#17)

Create: to produce something from nothing; to speak invisible things like thoughts, ideas and imaginations into existence. Words frame the thoughts that create your reality. (#4)

Criticize: to find fault with (#42)

Cultures: the habits, beliefs and traditions of a particular people (#45)

Current: the directional flow of water (#37)

Damaging: causing harm or loss to (#27)

Decorate: to make more attractive (#29)

Dedication: an act of setting apart for a special purpose (#41)

Define: to explain the meaning of (#73)

Deflate: take air out of (#34)

Dependable: capable of being trusted (#50)

Descriptions: written or spoken statements about something (#44)

Deserted: left without intending to return of (#34)

Design: to think up and plan out in the mind (#28)

Destiny: what happens to someone or something in the future (#36)

Detailed: including many small items or parts (#29)

Determination: firm or fixed intention (#36)

Determine: to come to a decision (#64)

Development: the state of or result of maturing and changing (#55)

Devoted: completely loyal (#40)

Diagonal: running from one corner to the opposite corner (#63)

Disaster: something that happens suddenly and causes suffering or loss (#69)

Disrupt: to interrupt the normal course of (#43)

Distinct: easy to notice or understand (#45)

Distracted: have attention drawn to something else (#43)

Distribute: to divide among many (#15)

Donate: to make a gift of (#46)

Drawn: to take out of (#62)

Drummond: a Scottish writer and clergyman (#74)

Effective: able to produce a desired result (#56)

Efficient: bringing about a desired result with little waste (#56)

Emerge: to come out or into view (#76)

Emotions: strong feelings along with physical reactions (#28)

Empathy: the understanding and sharing of the emotions of another person (#45)

Encounter: to meet or come face to face (#77)

Encourage: to give help or support to (#28)

Encouraging: giving hope or confidence to (#16)

Endanger: to expose to harm (#55)

Endured: put up with (#51)

Energy: ability to be active; strong action or effort (#62)

Enthusiasm: strong feeling in favor of something (#28)

Entire: complete in all parts (#76)

Entrepreneur: an individual who creates a new business (#74)

Environment: a person's physical surroundings (#28)

Eolic Energy: power created by the wind (#62)

Evaluate: to judge the value or condition of (#73)

Explore: to go into for purposes of discovery or adventure (#35)

Extend: to make longer or larger (#69)

Extensive: including or affecting many things (#55)

Extent: the distance or range that is covered (#55)

External: situated on or relating to the outside (#68)

Family: a household consisting of parents and children living together. Family forms culture and determines values. It should be a safe place. (#4)

Faithful: firm in devotion or support (#40)

Farmhand: a farm worker (#74)

Fixed Mindset: a mental attitude that is not willing to change (#32)

Flexible: easy to bend (#23)

Food chain: living things depending on each other for food (#54)

Forgiving: ready or willing to excuse an error or offense (#28)

Fossil fuels: a fuel formed in the earth from plant or animal remains (#62)

Fuel: substance that can be burned to produce power (#62)

Gain: an increase in amount (#50)

Generate: to cause to come into being (#62)

Generous: freely giving or sharing (#30)

Gentle: soft and delicate (#42)

Geothermal Energy: energy that uses heat from inside the earth (#62)

Gnawing: biting or chewing on with the teeth (#51)

Grit: strength of mind or spirit (#36)

Growth Mindset: a person's belief in the their own ability to learn and develop skills (#32)

Habit: usual way of behaving (#57)

Habitats: places where plants or animals naturally live and grow (#55)

Harsh: severe or cruel; not kind (#16)

Humble: teachable; not proud or arrogant (#22)

Humored: made to laugh (#51)

Hunch: a strong feeling concerning a future event or result (#21)

Hurdles: barriers or obstacles (#75)

Hydraulic Energy: energy that is operated or brought about by means of water (#62)

Identical: being exactly alike or equal (#70)

Imaginative: showing an ability to think of new and interesting ideas (#35)

Impact: a strong effect (#31)

Impassable: impossible to pass, cross or travel (#76)

Implies: suggests rather than says plainly (#41)

Improve: to make or become better (#27)

Incredible: too improbable to be believed (#36)

Infancy: a beginning or early period of existence (#18)

Inflate: to expand or increase with air (#34)

Influence: to affect in an indirect usually important way (#26)

Inspirational: something that is moving or felt with emotion (#61)

Instructions: outline of how something is to be done (#13)

Insult: an act or statement showing disrespect (#42)

Interacting: talking or doing things with other people (#61)

Internal: being within something; within the body (#21)

Invention: something that is created or produced for the first time (#28)

Inventor: a person who creates or produces new things (#59)

Irritated: made sensitive or sore (#49)

Items: things in a list or series (#58)

Judge: to form an opinion after careful consideration (#42)

Knit: to make clothes (#28)

Lack: to need or be without something (#21)

Leadership: to lead, administrate, manage, or to go before. It is the ability to influence others through words and deeds. (#4)

Lend: to give usually for a time (#46)

Life cycle: a series of stages someone/something passes through during their lifetime (#18)

Limits: boundary lines (#21)

Love: a personal decision to give the best you have for the wellbeing of another, independent of merit and without expecting anything in return. True love is unconditional (#4)

Loyal: showing true and constant support (#41)

Magnificent: very beautiful or impressive (#36)

Manage: to look after and make decisions about (#73)

Mature: fully grown or developed (#18)

Maximize: to make the most of (#72)

Maze: a confusing arrangement of paths or passages (#46)

Meerkats: an African mongoose; small burrowing animal (#15)

Menu: the dishes available for or served at a meal (#27)

Milkweed: a plant with milky juice and clusters for flowers (#76)

Mindful: keep in thoughts; aware (#60)

Mingle: to move among others within a group (#72)

Mini Workshop: a short session to teach others something (#33)

Mistreat: abuse; be mean to (#60)

Moderator: the chairman of a discussion group (#49)

Modest: descent in thought, conduct and dress; something smaller than others (#22)

Mold: to work and press into shape (#22)

Monarch Butterfly: a large orange and black American butterfly (#76)

Morals: principles of right and wrong in behavior (#22)

Non-renewable: not capable of being replaced (#62)

Nuclear fuels: fuel that provides nuclear energy as in power stations (#62)

Obstacle: something that stands in the way or opposes (#74)

Odds: conditions that make something difficult (#36)

Opportunities: chances for greater success (#75)

Optimistic: expecting good things to happen (#32)

Organizational: ability to put things in neat and structured arrangement (#57)

Origin: the point at which something begins (#72)

Original: not copied from anything else; the first (#71)

Participant: a person who takes part in something (#33)

Pattern: a model or guide for making something (#73)

Persevere: to keep trying to do something in spite of difficulties (#77)

Persistence: refusing to give up; continuing to do something (#36)

Personalities: human beings' unique qualities (#45)

Phases: steps or parts in a series of events (#18)

Phrase: a group of two or more words that express a single idea (#50)

Planet: any large heavenly body that orbits a star (#64)

Pleasant: having pleasing manners, behavior or appearance (#30)

Poeticized: to give a poetic quality to (#74)

Polite: showing courtesy or good manners (#21)

Possessions: things that are held by someone as property (#68)

Predators: animals that live mostly by killing and eating other animals (#36)

Prefer: to like better than another (#57)

Pressure: the need to get things done (#21)

Prioritize: to put in order based on importance (#73)

Prized: highly valued (#68)

Produce: to generate, to make, to yield or give results. Small things can produce great results. Inside every seed is the image of a plant, but not just one plant, acres of plants or trees. (#4)

Productive: having the power to yield in large amounts (#57)

Profitable: producing a benefit or monetary gain (#59)

Projectile: something thrown or shot especially from a weapon (#74)

Promise: a statement by a person about their future actions (#50)

Purposefully: having a clear intention or aim (#19)

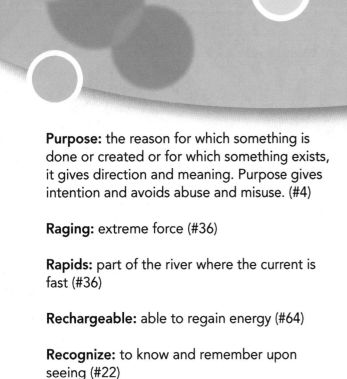

Purpose: the reason for which something is done or created or for which something exists, it gives direction and meaning. Purpose gives intention and avoids abuse and misuse. (#4)

Raging: extreme force (#36)

Rapids: part of the river where the current is fast (#36)

Rechargeable: able to regain energy (#64)

Recognize: to know and remember upon seeing (#22)

Recycling: adapting to a new use (#58)

Referee: a person who makes sure players follow the rules of a game or sport (#49)

Reflection: an image as if by a mirror (#57)

Reflect: show image like in a mirror (#57)

Regardless: in spite of something that might be a problem (#72)

Relate: to have a relationship or to connect (#37)

Relationships: the state of being related or connected (#28)

Reliable: fit to be trusted (#41)

Renewable: capable of being replaced (#62)

Represent: to act for or in place of (#44)

Re-purpose: to give a new purpose or use to (#58)

Requires: something that is necessary to succeed (#64)

Respect: high or special regard (#20)

Review: to look at or study again (#28)

Role: the job done by a member of a team or family (#13)

Rooting: encouraging a contestant or team; cheering (#37)

Routine: a usual way and order of doing something (#35)

Satisfaction: content; the condition of being well pleased (#15)

Sceneries: pleasant outdoor scenes or views (#64)

Scheduled: set on a timetable; put on the calendar (#72)

Sculpted: carved or molded into a particular shape (#22)

Sensitivity: taking care to do what is best for another; careful to not hurt others (#47)

Signature: the name of a person written by that person (#43)

Similar: having qualities in common (#21)

Sincere: having or showing honesty (#41)

Skills: developed or acquired abilities (#14)

Sorry: feeling sorrow or regret (#30)

Stage: a specific time period in the development of something (#18)

Statement: something stated or written in a formal way (#33)

Strained: not easy or natural (#35)

Strategy: a careful plan or method (#48)

Stung: (sting) sharp quick prick, bite or pain caused by an object, plants, insect or other animal (#26)

Styles: qualities that are felt to be very respectable or fashionable (#45)

Succeed: to turn out well; to achieve a desired result (#14)

Surroundings: the conditions or things around an individual; environment (#34)

Survive: to remain alive; to continue to exist (#36)

Talent: unusual natural ability (#33)

Tasks: pieces of work that have been assigned (#73)

Tidal Energy: a hydro-power that transforms the movement of tides into electricity (#62)

Transformed: changed completely into something new (#59)

Trial: hardship or problem (#51)

Trustworthy: worthy of confidence (#41)

Tugged: pulled hard (#51)

Uncomfortable: feeling discomfort or uneasiness (#47)

Unique: being the only one of its kind (#36)

Unreachable: impossible to get to or get out (#73)

Untangle: to remove a tangle from; to straighten out (#48)

Vaccinations: preparations that are given usually by injections to protect against a certain disease (#61)

Value: worth, usefulness or importance (#19)

Viewpoint: a way of looking or thinking about something (#75)

Volunteer: a person who does something by free choice without expecting to be paid (#28)

Wear: the damage done to something by its use (#34)

Well-being: state of being happy and healthy (#26)

Work: activity involving mental or physical effort done in order to achieve a purpose, it is to serve; to share your unique strengths, abilities, knowledge and ideas with those around you, generally creating satisfaction within you. (#4)

Yanks: pulls suddenly or forcefully (#48)

GENERATION WHY

INSPIRE. REVEAL. PURSUE.

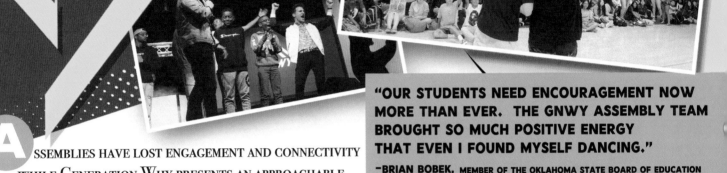

ASSEMBLIES HAVE LOST ENGAGEMENT AND CONNECTIVITY WHILE GENERATION WHY PRESENTS AN APPROACHABLE WAY TO DISCUSS SOME OF THE MOST DIFFICULT TOPICS STUDENTS ARE FACING IN THE REALM OF TRAUMA.

GENERATION WHY'S BLEND OF HIGH ENERGY, INSPIRING SPEAKING AND RELATABLE CREATIVE ARTS HAVE STUDENTS AND TEACHERS ON THE EDGE OF THEIR SEATS READY TO RECEIVE CHANGE AND HOPE.

HOPE EVOKES CHANGE AND CHANGE CAN BE THE TURNING POINT THAT MOVES A HEART IN A POSITIVE DIRECTION. GNWY USES RAPPERS, DANCERS, SPOKEN WORD ARTISTS AND MOTIVATIONAL SPEAKERS, THAT ENCOURAGE DIVERSITY, CULTURAL RELEVANCE, UNITY, AND SCHOOL BODY, STUDENT WIDE EMPOWERMENT.

THROUGH AN ASSEMBLY / PERFORMANCE / PRESENTATION, YOU ARE MOVED NOT ONLY PHYSICALLY, BUT EMOTIONALLY TOWARD A HEALTHIER YOU THROUGH CONVERSATIONS, RELATIONSHIPS AND ULTIMATELY, A HEALTHIER SCHOOL COMMUNITY.

> "OUR STUDENTS NEED ENCOURAGEMENT NOW MORE THAN EVER. THE GNWY ASSEMBLY TEAM BROUGHT SO MUCH POSITIVE ENERGY THAT EVEN I FOUND MYSELF DANCING."
> —BRIAN BOBEK, MEMBER OF THE OKLAHOMA STATE BOARD OF EDUCATION

> "GENERATION WHY IS A BURST OF ENERGY AND ENCOURAGEMENT. THEY ARE CREATIVE STORYTELLERS AND ARTISTS THAT HAVE TURNED THEIR TRAUMAS INTO TRIUMPHS AND NOW USE THEIR GIFTS AND TALENTS TO INSPIRE TODAY'S YOUTH! I AM SO GRATEFUL FOR THEIR LEADERSHIP IN OUR COMMUNITY."
> —ASHLEY HOGGATT, PRINCIPAL, DD KIRKLAND ELEMENTARY; BOARD MEMBER, OKLAHOMA ADMINISTRATOR FOR ELEMENTARY PRINCIPALS

WWW.PURSUEYOURWHY.ORG

CONTACT: GNWY@FIGHTFORTHEFORGOTTEN.ORG

EMPOWERED BY:

80